麦格希 中英双语阅读文库

探险之旅

第3辑

【美】罗莉·波利佐罗斯 (Lori Polydoros) ●主编

张琳琳　王雨红●译

麦格希中英双语阅读文库编委会●编

全国百佳图书出版单位
吉林出版集团股份有限公司

图书在版编目（CIP）数据

探险之旅. 第3辑 / (美) 罗莉・波利佐罗斯 (Lori Polydoros) 主编；张琳琳，王雨红译；麦格希中英双语阅读文库编委会编. -- 2版. -- 长春：吉林出版集团股份有限公司, 2018.3（2022.1重印）
（麦格希中英双语阅读文库）
ISBN 978-7-5581-4772-2

Ⅰ. ①探… Ⅱ. ①罗… ②张… ③王… ④麦… Ⅲ. ①英语—汉语—对照读物②故事—作品集—美国—现代 Ⅳ. ①H319.4：I

中国版本图书馆CIP数据核字(2018)第046400号

探险之旅　第3辑

编：麦格希中英双语阅读文库编委会
插　　画：齐　航　李延霞
责任编辑：王芳芳
封面设计：冯冯翼
开　　本：660mm × 960mm　1/16
字　　数：231千字
印　　张：10.25
版　　次：2018年3月第2版
印　　次：2022年1月第2次印刷

出　　版：吉林出版集团股份有限公司
发　　行：吉林出版集团外语教育有限公司
地　　址：长春市福祉大路5788号龙腾国际大厦B座7层
邮编：130011
电　　话：总编办：0431-81629929
发行部：0431-81629927　0431-81629921(Fax)
印　　刷：北京一鑫印务有限责任公司

ISBN 978-7-5581-4772-2　　定价：38.00元

前言 *PREFACE*

英国思想家培根说过：阅读使人深刻。阅读的真正目的是获取信息，开拓视野和陶冶情操。从语言学习的角度来说，学习语言若没有大量阅读就如隔靴搔痒，因为阅读中的语言是最丰富、最灵活、最具表现力、最符合生活情景的，同时读物中的情节、故事引人入胜，进而能充分调动读者的阅读兴趣，培养读者的文学修养，至此，语言的学习水到渠成。

“麦格希中英双语阅读文库”在世界范围内选材，涉及科普、社会文化、文学名著、传奇故事、成长励志等多个系列，充分满足英语学习者课外阅读之所需，在阅读中学习英语、提高能力。

◎难度适中

本套图书充分照顾读者的英语学习阶段和水平，从读者的阅读兴趣出发，以难易适中的英语语言为立足点，选材精心、编排合理。

◎精品荟萃

本套图书注重经典阅读与实用阅读并举。既包含国内外脍炙人口、耳熟能详的美文，又包含科普、人文、故事、励志类等多学科的精彩文章。

◎功能实用

本套图书充分体现了双语阅读的功能和优势，充分考虑到读者课外阅读的方便，超出核心词表的词汇均出现在使其意义明显的语境之中，并标注释义。

鉴于编者水平有限，凡不周之处，谬误之处，皆欢迎批评教正。

我们真心地希望本套图书承载的文化知识和英语阅读的策略对提高读者的英语著作欣赏水平和英语运用能力有所裨益。

丛书编委会

Contents

1

The Buffalo Hunt

Preparing for the Hunt

Wind-in-the-Treetops was going out on the yearly *buffalo* hunt. Last year, he had followed the hunters with the women and other children. As a baby, he had been tucked on top of the packs that his mother's *pony* carried. As an older boy, he had had to share space on the pack ponies with several other children.

But now he had a pony of his own.Wind-in-the-Treetops was going to ride with the men this year. He was so proud! His

猎捕野牛

狩猎前的准备

树梢之风就要参加一年一度的野牛猎捕了。去年，他就已经和女人还有孩子们一起，跟在猎手们后面，拾取猎物了。很小的时候，他就被母亲放在马背上的摇篮里。等到稍大一些的时候，他就和其他的孩子们一起坐在马背上。

而现在他已经拥有了属于自己的马。今年，树梢之风就要跟成年的男子们一起狩猎了。他真是太自豪了！而弟弟们却只有羡慕的份儿，只能跟在猎手们的后面。

buffalo *n.* 野牛　　pony *n.* 矮种马

younger brothers, who still had to stay behind, *envied* him.

"I won't tire out my pony by riding him before the hunt," he said. "I will walk and lead him. Then he will be fresh for the chase."

Wind-in-the-Treetops wanted his pony to run fast after the buffaloes. He did not ride his pony for four days. During those four days, the medicine men and the hunters prayed for the success of the hunt. In the medicine lodge, they held the sacred buffalo dance.

The young men dressed in buffalo skins. They put on buffalo masks with horns. Then they danced until they were so tired that they fell down. When one man fell, the others would *pretend* he was a buffalo they had killed. They would pretend to skin and cut up the buffalo. *Meanwhile*, another man picked up the mask and started

---

他说："狩猎活动开始前，我可不能骑在我的小马身上，那会累坏它的。我自己走，牵着它。那样追捕的时候它才能有力气。"

树梢之风想让他的马在追逐野牛的时候精力充沛。因此，狩猎前他让小马休息了四天。在这四天里，巫师和猎手们做了法事，祈祷他们能满载而归。猎手们在神庙里跳祭祀野牛的舞蹈。

青年男子披上野牛皮，戴上有角的野牛面具。然后一直跳到筋疲力尽，摔倒在地。每当有人倒在地上，大家就会把他假想为被猎取的野牛，假装剥牛皮，切牛肉。这时，会有人拾起他的面具，接替他跳舞。部落里的人相信这种舞蹈会引来附近的野牛。他们日夜不停地跳着，直到听到牛群的消息。

---

envy *v.* 羡慕

pretend *v.* 假装

meanwhile *adv.* 同时

dancing. The tribe believed that this dance brought the buffaloes near. They danced night and day until news of the *herds* came.

The Hunt Begins

The men started out on the hunt before dawn. The women and children followed a short distance behind. The hunters rode in a line across the *prairie*. A few men led the hunt. No one was allowed to go ahead of these leaders. Men who had two ponies rode the slower one and led the faster one. Men who had only one pony, like Wind-in-the-Treetops, walked, to keep their ponies fresh.

The boy became very tired on the long walk. But he would not tire his pony. So a kind old man named Eagle Chief said to Wind-in-the-Treetops, "Young friend, come and ride with me on my pony. You

---

狩猎开始了

猎手们在黎明前动身去狩猎。女人和孩子们紧跟在他们身后。猎手们一个跟着一个在草原上行进，其中有几个是领头人，他们走在大家前面。拥有两匹马的猎手们骑着跑得慢的那匹，牵着快马。而像树梢之风这样只拥有一匹马的猎手为了保存马的体力，就只能走路。

经过这么长的路途，树梢之风感到很疲惫。即使再怎么累，他也不会骑上他的马。于是，善良的老首领鹰对他说："小伙子，坐到我的马上吧。你把我的另外那匹马和你的马牵在一起。"树梢之风高兴地谢了首领。

---

herd *n.* 牛群

prairie *n.* 大草原

can lead your pony with my spare pony." Wind-in-the-Treetops was very glad and grateful.

After a long, long march, the *scouts* returned. They said, "We see the buffaloes." Then every man got on his swiftest pony. The leaders of the hunt directed them to circle around the buffaloes. The hunters went very quietly so the buffaloes would not hear them.

Wind-in-the-Treetops saw the dark shapes of the buffaloes against the edge of the sky. He was so excited that he could hardly sit still. He wanted to *dash* on ahead, but that was *forbidden*. Going ahead might *stampede* the herd and spoil the hunt for the whole tribe.

走了很久之后，负责侦察的猎手们回来了。他们说：“我们发现野牛了。”很快，所有的人都骑上了马，捕猎的领头人指挥他们围成一个圈，把野牛围在里面。猎手们的动作非常轻，怕惊动这群野牛。

看到了天边黑压压的成群的野牛，树梢之风激动地再也坐不住了。他很想冲到前面去，可却不能这么做。那样会吓跑野牛，整个部落的狩猎就会毁于一旦。所以，所有的猎手都在小心翼翼地悄悄接近牛群。

---

scout *n.* 侦察者
forbid *v.* 禁止
dash *v.* 猛冲
stampede *v.* 使惊跑

So the hunters went on very softly and ***cautiously***.

Suddenly the buffaloes caught sight of them. Their ***shaggy*** heads lifted, and they ran as fast as deer. Their slim legs seemed so small, and their great heads and chests seemed so big. Now the leaders let every man ride as fast as he could.

All the men dashed ahead, trying to catch the buffaloes. Wind-in-the-Treetops's pony was fast. It carried him along with the lead hunters. He was dangerously close to the terrified buffaloes.

Surrounded on all sides, the buffaloes tried to fight their way out of the circle. But the men shot with wonderful strength and swiftness.

突然，这些野牛发现了他们，抬起乱蓬蓬的头，急速飞奔。它们的细腿看起来很小，头和胸却似乎很大。这时，领头人吩咐大家赶紧追。

大家都快马加鞭地往前冲，追猎这些野牛。树梢之风的马跑得很快，带着他追上了领头的猎手们，追上了那些可怕的野牛。

野牛们看到无路可逃，拼命地想要逃过猎手们的围猎。然而，猎手们射出了一支又一支的利箭，随即射伤和射死了一头接着一头的野牛。猎手们并不理那些倒在地上的牛，而是继续追猎其他的牛。他们知道，部落的其他人就跟在后面，女人们会把自己丈夫和儿子猎杀的

---

cautiously *adv.* 小心地

shaggy *adj.* 蓬乱的

surround *v.* 包围

One great beast after another fell wounded or dead. The men let them lie and continued their *chase*. They knew that the rest of the tribe was close behind. Each woman would claim the buffalo shot by her husband or son.

After the Hunt

Wind-in-the-Treetops rode on until he had shot the very last arrow from his *quiver*. The last of the buffaloes had *disappeared* from view. He turned back very slowly. His pony was tired. He was tired, too. He was so tired that he could hardly hold up his head. All the way back, he saw women skinning buffaloes and cutting up the meat.

Pretty soon he saw his younger brother shouting, leaping, and

---

野牛收起来。

狩猎结束了

树梢之风射光了所有的箭才回来。幸存的那些野牛跑得看不见了，他才慢慢地返回。他的马累坏了，他也累坏了，累得连抬头的力气都快没有了。回来时，他看到了那些女人们都在剥牛皮，切牛肉。

很快，他就看见了弟弟在欢呼雀跃，手中挥动着剥牛皮的刀。母亲正拿着刀，俯身看着一头大野牛。树梢之风跳下马，所有的疲惫都消失得

---

chase *n.* 追逐

quiver *n.* 箭筒

disappear *v.* 消失

waving his skinning knife. His mother was bending over a huge buffalo with her knife. Wind-in-the-Treetops *sprang* from his pony. He forgot all about being tired.

"Did I kill it, Mother?" he cried. "Did I kill it?"

"Yes," said his mother. "Here is your arrow, which I pulled from it. We will have meat for the winter and fine, warm fur. I am very proud that my son has become a great hunter."

No one was happier than Wind-in-the-Treetops. He wanted to shout out loud. He saw the racks full of drying red meat, and he thought *joyfully*, "I killed a buffalo! Our camp will have plenty of food this winter."

无影无踪了。

他喊道："是我射死的吗，妈妈？是我吗？"

母亲答道："是的，我在它身上拔出了你的箭。我们有肉和暖和的皮毛可以过冬了。我很自豪，我的儿子成为一名出色的猎手了。"

树梢之风高兴极了。他想大声喊出来。他仿佛看到了一袋袋风干了的野牛肉，他高兴地想着："我猎到了一头野牛，家里有充足的食物过冬了。"

---

spring *v.* 跳　　joyfully *adv.* 高兴地

2

Sally's Secret *Ambition*

Chapter One

The War Between the States had begun last year. The North was fighting the South. Fathers were fighting sons; brothers were fighting each other. Sally was thankful as she set the table that her family had not been torn apart by this terrible war.

Sally could smell the bacon cooking in the kitchen. She knew that she and her family were lucky. They had enough food to eat. Other

萨莉心中的志向

第一章

国内战争在去年爆发了。北方与南方对抗。父子相残，兄弟操戈。萨莉坐在桌前，很庆幸她的家庭没有在这场可怕的战争中四分五裂。

萨莉能闻到厨房里培根的香味。她知道自己和家人很幸运。他们能有充足的食物。很多家庭现在都食不果腹。战争一打响，食品的价格就在飞

ambition *n.* 志向

families did not. The prices for food had gone way up when the war started.

Many families had already lost sons and brothers to the war. Sally was thankful that her father and brother had not gone to fight.

Sally's father was a *surgeon*. He took care of soldiers who were hurt fighting in the war, and Sally's brother Alexander helped him. Sally wanted to help her father, too. She had watched him closely over the years. She practiced what she learned by *bandaging* wounds on her dolls. Now she could help *injured* animals. But her mother discouraged her interest in being a doctor. She would say, "I need your help at home. Besides, no man wants a surgeon for a wife."

速上涨。

这场战争使许多家庭失去了儿子和兄弟。萨莉很庆幸父亲和哥哥都没有参加战争。

萨莉的父亲是一位外科医生。他照顾那些在战争中受伤的士兵，哥哥亚历山大在为父亲帮忙。萨莉也想帮父亲。这些年她在父亲身边耳濡目染，总是在玩偶身上练习包扎伤口。现在，她已经能照顾那些受伤的动物了。但母亲总是不希望她做医生。她会说："我需要你在家帮忙。再说，没有人愿意找一名外科医生做妻子。"

---

surgeon *n.* 外科医生
bandage *v.* 用绷带包扎
injured *adj.* 受伤的

Sally finished setting the table for breakfast. Her mother brought in the food and put it on the dining table. Sally rang a small silver bell let her father and brother know that breakfast was ready.

"Good morning, Sally," said her father as he walked into the dining room. He didn't look as he had been up for hours *operating*, thought Sally. Her father seemed to love his work even though it was difficult. With the war, his work had him awake at all hours of the day and night.

Father gave Sally a kiss on the *forehead* before taking his seat at the head of the table. "What a lovely breakfast, Virginia," he said to his wife as he served himself. Then he passed the eggs to Alexander.

萨莉布置完早餐的餐桌。母亲端上来食物，放在餐桌上。萨莉摇动小银铃，通知父亲和哥哥，早餐准备好了。

“早上好，萨莉，”父亲走进餐厅说。萨莉想，他看起来并不像熬了几个小时做手术的样子。虽然很辛苦，父亲看起来还是很热爱自己的工作。由于战争，他夜以继日地工作。

父亲吻了一下萨莉的额头，然后坐在了餐桌的一端。“早餐很可口啊，维吉妮亚，”他边吃边对妻子说。然后，把鸡蛋递给亚历山大。

---

operate *v.* 做手术　　forhead *n.* 额头

"Thank you, Father," said Alexander, "but I don't think I can eat this morning."

"Are you ill?" asked Virginia. Sally saw the worry on her mother's face. Their neighbors had lost their baby to illness earlier that year, and Sally's mother feared the worst when someone in their family became ill.

"The boy's not ili, Virginia," Sally's father said in a booming voice. Then he ***chuckled***. "I'm afraid our son still cannot stand the sight of an operation," he said. "He almost ***fainted*** early this morning at the field hospital while was working on a boy's badly wounded leg."

Alexander got the chance to do what Sally dreamed of doing.

"谢谢，爸爸，"亚历山大说，"但我今天早晨吃不下。"

"不舒服吗？"维吉妮亚问。萨莉看到了母亲脸上的担忧。今年早些时候，他们邻居家的孩子生病死掉了，萨莉的母亲最担心家里有人生病。

"孩子没生病，维吉妮亚，"父亲用低沉的声音说。随后他笑着说："恐怕我们的儿子还不适应见到手术的场面。今天凌晨，我在战地医院为一名腿伤严重的男孩截肢时，他差点晕过去。"

亚历山大得到了萨莉梦寐以求的机会，但却不想做外科医生。当意识

---

chuckle *v.* 低声轻笑

faint *v.* 昏厥

But Alexander wanted to be anything but a surgeon. Sally's anger had risen when she realized that. It was not fair. Sally dreamed that one day she would help people as her father did. But she kept that dream a secret. She knew her mother would dig her heels in and say, "No man would want a doctor for a wife and that's that."

Chapter Two

After breakfast, Sally cleared the table and washed the dishes. Then she dusted the books in her father's study. She knew all his books by heart. When she was young, her father let her look at the pictures of the human body. He taught her the names of all the bones and organs. As Sally got older, her free time was spent ***sneaking*** into the study to read his books again and again. She

到这点时，萨莉感到愤愤不平。真是太不公平了。萨莉梦想着有一天能像父亲一样救治病患。不过，她把这个梦想藏在心中。她知道母亲一定不会同意，她会说：“没有人会娶医生做妻子之类的话。”

第二章

早餐后，萨莉收拾了餐桌，清洗了盘子。然后她就去父亲的书房，清扫书上的灰尘。父亲所有的书她都了然于心。小时候，父亲总是让她看人体的图片。然后教给她所有骨骼和器官的名称。长大后，她所有的闲暇时间都用来溜进父亲的书房，一遍遍地阅读他的那些书籍。她希望有一天，

sneak *v.* 偷偷地走；溜

hoped that one day she could *persuade* her parents to let her help at the field hospital. She just had to think of a way to do it, *otherwise* her life's ambition might have to remain a dream.

Sally had been secretly watching her father do operations. She hid so he would not know she was there. At first, the sight of blood had *upset* her. But she reminded herself that her father was saving a life. Being able to save someone's life seemed noble to Sally.

Sally watched her father's operations from her secret hiding place in a closet. She snuck away from her *chores* every chance she got. She feared getting caught sneaking around. She did not want to upset her mother. She wanted to respect her wishes, but becoming a doctor was important to Sally. When the day came for

---

她能说服父母允许她到战地医院帮忙。她得想个办法出来，否则她毕生的志向就有可能化为泡影。

萨莉曾经偷偷地观察过父亲做手术。她藏了起来，这样就不会被父亲发现了。一开始，看见血，她会不舒服。但她提醒自己，父亲是在挽救生命。救死扶伤在萨丽心中是神圣的。

萨丽悄悄地藏在壁橱里偷看父亲做手术。一有机会，她就会从家务活中抽出身来，偷偷溜出来。她害怕被母亲逮到。不想辜负母亲的期望。她想尊重母亲的意愿，可是，做医生对萨莉来说很重要。萨莉想在说服父母

---

persuade *v.* 说服

otherwise *conj.* 不然

upset *v.* 使不快

chore *n.* 日常事务

Sally to persuade her parents, Sally wanted to be ready for it. Sally continued watching her father, and wrote down what she saw him do in a secret notebook that she kept hidden under her bed.

Chapter Three

One afternoon, Sally was alone at home doing the *laundry*. Her mother was at the home of a neighbor, helping other women make bandages from old *sheets*.

Sally heard *cannon* shots in the distance. Another battle, she thought. More wounded soldiers. She pictured her father and brother working at the field hospital, tending to the wounded soldiers.

Sally gathered up the clean, wet clothes from the laundry *tub* to take them outside to the clothesline. The clothes were piled so high

---

前，做好准备。她继续偷偷地观察父亲做手术，并把看到的东西记在一个秘密的笔记本上，她把本子藏在床下。

第三章

一天下午，她独自在家洗衣服。母亲去了邻居家，帮其他的妇女把旧床单做成绷带。

萨莉听到了远处的炮声。她想，又一场战役打起来了。会有很多伤员。她想象着父亲和哥哥在战地医院忙着照顾那些受伤的士兵。

萨莉从洗衣桶里拿出那些干净的湿衣服，要把它们挂在外面的晾衣绳上。衣服在她怀里堆得很高，她根本没有看见一个士兵正向她走过来。士

---

laundry *n.* 洗衣物，洗衣物的活
sheet *n.* 被单
cannon *n.* 大炮
tub *n.* 桶

in her arms that she did not see the soldier coming toward her. She nearly jumped out of her skin when he called to her. ***Startled***, she dropped the clean laundry on the ground.

The soldier was wounded, but the cut was not too deep. Sally saw that blood was ***soaking*** through the ***sleeve*** on the soldier's uniform. She ripped one of the sheets and ***wrapped*** it tightly around his wound to stop the bleeding.

"Please, could you help my friend, John," begged the soldier. "He got shot in the leg."

Sally ran into the house and grabbed her father's spare medical bag. She took the ripped sheet and got some water from the well, then followed the soldier down the road. As they hurried along, the

---

兵叫她时，她吓了一大跳。慌忙中，她把洗干净的衣服掉到了地上。

这名士兵受伤了，但伤口不是太深。萨莉看见血浸湿了士兵制服的袖子。她撕了一条床单，紧紧地包扎了他的伤口，为他止住流血。

“请问，你能帮帮我的朋友约翰吗？”士兵哀求道。“他腿上中枪了。”

萨莉冲进房子，抓起父亲的备用医疗袋。拿着撕成条的床单，从井里打了一些水，然后跟着士兵沿公路跑去。路上，士兵介绍了自己。他叫乔

---

startle *v.* 使吓一跳　　soak *v.* 浸透
sleeve *n.* 袖子　　wrap *v.* 包扎

soldier introduced himself. His name was George, and he was not much older than Sally.

George's friend was not far away. John was sitting against a tree, his leg bleeding badly. Sally gave the boy some water, then turned to treat his wound. She washed away his blood with the water, but the blood *swiftly* covered the wound again. She saw enough to know that a *lead* bullet was not very deep in his leg.

Sally tore a bandage from the sheet, then took the *forceps* from her father's bag. She *gripped* the end of the bullet with the forceps and pulled it from John's leg. Next, Sally quickly wrapped the bandage tightly around the wound to stop the bleeding. The

---

治，比萨莉大不了多少。

乔治的朋友离他们并不远。约翰靠坐在一棵树下，他的腿出了很多血。萨莉喂他喝了一些水，然后开始处理他的伤口。她用水为约翰清洗伤口上的血，但血液很快又再次覆盖住了伤口。她仔细观察，发现他腿上的铅弹不是很深。

萨莉从床单上扯下一条作绷带，然后从父亲的医药袋里拿出镊子。用镊子夹住子弹的尾部，取出了约翰腿上的子弹。紧接着，萨莉迅速地用绷

---

swiftly *adv.* 迅速地
forcep *n.* 镊子
lead *n.* 铅
grip *v.* 抓紧

pressure from the bandage would keep him from losing too much blood and becoming ***unconscious***.

Once Sally was sure the bleeding had slowed, she would have to take the boy to her father.

George watched Sally work. "You bandaged his leg as well as a doctor would have," he said, ***impressed*** with Sally's skill. "Where did you learn to do that?"

"My father is a surgeon," said Sally.

"He must be very proud of you," said George. Sally hoped so, but she knew her mother would be angry if she found Sally covered in blood, wrapping bandages around men's legs.

带裹紧伤口止血。绷带的压力会避免他失血过多，出现昏迷现象。

一旦萨莉确定流血止住了，她就必须带约翰去父亲那里。

乔治看着萨莉处置伤口，说："你跟医生包扎得一样好，"萨莉的技术给他留下了深刻的印象。"你从哪里学来的？"

"我父亲是外科医生，"萨莉说。

"他一定很为你骄傲，"乔治说。萨莉真希望是这样，但她知道母亲要是知道她满身是血，用绷带包扎男人的腿，一定会生气。

unconscious *adj.* 无意识地

impress *v.* 给……留下深刻的印象

Sally was so lost in thought and so focused on her work that she did not hear her father and brother as they came up behind her.

"You did a good job with that bandage, Sally," said her father.

"Better than I could do," admitted Alexander.

Sally *appreciated* the praise. Then she saw her mother walking toward them.

Chapter Four

"What is going on here?" Sally's mother demanded. "Sally! Are you hurt?"

"It looks like we have another doctor in the family," explained Sally's father.

Virginia's face turned *sour*. "Look at your dress. It's *filthy*!"

萨莉陷入沉思中，专注地思考着她的工作，并没有发现父亲和哥哥已经走到了她身后。

"你用绷带包扎得很好，萨莉，"父亲说。

"比我包得还好。"亚历山大也说。

萨莉听到赞扬很高兴。然后她看到母亲向他们走过来。

第四章

"这儿发生什么事了？"母亲问道，"萨莉！你受伤了吗？"

"看来我们家里又出了个医生，"萨莉的父亲解释说。

维吉妮亚生气了。"看看你的裙子。太脏了！"

---

appreciate *v.* 感激

sour *adj.* 不快的

filthy *adj.* 肮脏的

"Maybe Sally can help you at the field hospital instead of me," suggested Alexander.

"I need Sally at home," Sally's mother insisted. "She has chores to do."

"Mother," Sally began ***tentatively***, "I have been secretly watching Father work for years. I know what to do and what would be expected of me. I have dreamed of being a surgeon. Please let me help Father."

Sally watched as a range of emotions raced across both her parents' faces—fear, anger at having been ***deceived***, and even a bit of pride.

"或许萨莉可以代替我到战地医院帮你的忙，"亚历山大说。

"我需要萨莉待在家里，"母亲坚持说。"她得做家务。"

"妈妈，"萨莉试着鼓起勇气说，"我已经偷偷地看着父亲工作好多年了。我了解医务工作，知道自己应该做什么。我想成为一名外科医生。请让我去父亲那里帮忙吧。"

萨丽注意到父母脸上一闪而过的复杂情绪——预想到的担忧，气愤，甚至还有着些许的骄傲。

---

tentatively *adv.* 试验性地

deceive *v.* 欺骗

"I don't know, Sally," Virginia said as she started to walk toward the house.

Sally's father invited the young soldiers to the house so he could check their wounds. Once that was done, Virginia offered to cook a meal for all of them. Sally helped her mother prepare and serve the food. They even served a pie for dessert.

The men were grateful for the home-cooked meal as well as to Sally for bandaging their wounds. After saying their thanks and goodbyes, they left to *rejoin* their *troop*.

"I'll clear the table," offered Alexander, eager to stay away from the field hospital.

"我没想到，萨莉，"维吉妮亚边说边朝家走。

萨莉的父亲把士兵们请到家中，为他们检查伤口。之后，维吉妮亚为他们准备了丰盛的食物。萨莉帮母亲准备食物。他们甚至还吃了馅饼作为饭后甜点。

士兵们很感谢维吉妮亚为他们准备了家常菜，也很感谢萨莉为他们包扎了伤口。道谢和告别后，他们动身去与部队会合。

"我来收拾桌子，"亚历山大主动说，他渴望离开医院。

---

rejoin *v.* 重返

troop *n.* 军队

"Sally, would you like to come to the field hospital with me?" asked her father.

Sally looked to her mother. Virginia's *expression* said everything. She was not pleased, but she loved her daughter too much to build a *fence* around her dream.

Sally gave her mother another long look, and then said yes to her father. Sally's mother helped her find *suitable* clothes for her new work. She ended up wearing some of Alexander's clothes. There were changes going on in their country, and changes at home as well.

"萨丽，你愿意来战地医院帮我吗？" 父亲问。

萨丽看了一眼母亲。维吉妮亚的表情说明了一切。她不是很高兴，但她太爱女儿了，不能打破她的梦想。

萨莉看了母亲很久，然后答应了父亲。母亲帮她准备了适合医生穿的衣服。最后她穿着亚历山大的衣服走了。他们的国家正在经历变革，家庭也在经历变革。

---

expression *n.* 表情
fence *n.* 栅栏；障碍
suitable *adj.* 适合的

3

The Great Gallardo's Books

One Boring Saturday

Raindrops *splattered* the *asphalt* like a million *exploding firecrackers*. Miguel lined up toothpicks in the shape of a rocket ship on the counter. Working at his family's sandwich shop was not Miguel's idea of an exciting Saturday afternoon. Neither was doing homework.

伟大的盖拉多的魔法书

一个无聊的星期六

雨滴噼噼啪啪地溅落在柏油马路上，就好像是放响了无数的鞭炮。米格尔用牙签在柜台上摆了一艘火箭飞船。在这么美好的星期六下午，米格尔并不想在家里的三明治店帮忙，他也不想写作业。他得写一篇议论文，周一就要交。当然了，他甚至还没开始动笔写呢。

splatter *v.* 啪嗒啪嗒地落下

asphalt *n.* 沥青；柏油

explode *v.* 爆炸

firecracker *n.* 鞭炮

He had an essay due on Monday, and, of course, he hadn't even started!

"It's slow now," Miguel's mom said. "Go start your essay."

"It's too hard." Miguel *munched* the last *pickle* from the *jar*. "I can't write an essay about 'Reading Is an Adventure'."

"That doesn't sound so bad," Miguel's mom said.

"It does to me."

"Peel these." She slid a box of *cucumbers* over to him. "Or start your essay."

"Not much of a choice," Miguel thought.

"Fine, I'll do the essay." He dragged himself to the backroom and

---

"现在不忙了，"米格尔的妈妈说。"去写你的作文吧。"

"太难了。"米格尔嚼着从坛子里拿出的最后一块泡菜说。"我写不出'阅读是历险'这样的作文。"

"听起来这个题目不那么难写，"米格尔的妈妈说。

"我觉得很难。"

妈妈把一大箱黄瓜放到他跟前说。"把这些黄瓜皮削了。要不，你就去写作文。"

"这根本就没有什么选择的余地嘛，"米格尔想。

---

munch *v.* 用力咀嚼
pickle *n.* 泡菜
jar *n.* 坛子
cucumber *n.* 黄瓜

plopped down on a box. He stared at the lines on his paper. His mind was empty, like the pickle jar."How could reading be an adventure? "

The Loft

A tall, red ladder stood along the wall and Miguel wandered over to it. Miguel's mom used the ladder to reach the high boxes in the storage room. The ladder was so old that strips of red paint *peeled* off the wooden *rungs*. Miguel put his foot on the first rung and looked up — a loft he'd never noticed!

"好吧，我这就去写作文。"他极不情愿地走到后屋，一屁股坐到一只大箱子上。他盯着作文纸上的那些横线。脑子里就像刚才那个泡菜坛子一样，空空如也。"阅读怎么可能是历险呢？"

阁楼

米格尔看到墙边倚放着一把红色的大梯子，就朝它走过去。米格尔的妈妈用它去取储藏室里放在最顶上的那些箱子。梯子很旧了，木头梯级上的红漆都一片片地脱落了。米格尔登上了第一个梯阶，抬头向上望——这里竟然有一个他从没注意到的阁楼！

---

plop *v.* 使身子沉重地倒下
peel *v.* 剥去
rung *n.* 梯级，（梯子的）横档

Miguel tugged himself quickly up the ladder. Crack! The *topmost* rung *snapped*. Miguel began to slide.

His heart raced. Red paint chips fluttered down onto his hair like confetti. Miguel caught his foot on a rung and pushed off hard, leaping up into the loft. He made it!

Miguel found dusty boxes stacked to the ceiling, old magazines and newspapers littering the ground, and a sagging, purple couch. Old posters plastered the walls-posters that even in their faded condition, screamed with color and interesting designs. One read "The Great Gallardo! "It showed a hooded figure beneath an arch of shooting stars. A *glittery* black chest with a lock fit *snugly* up against

---

米格尔快速地沿着梯子向上爬。啪的一声！最顶上的梯级断了。米格尔脚下一滑。

他的心吓得怦怦直跳。一片片的红漆像婚礼中的五彩纸屑一样，飘落到他的头发上。米格尔用脚蹬住梯级，使劲向上一蹿，跳上了阁楼。他上来了。

米格尔看到了一大堆一直堆到天花板的布满灰尘的箱子，散落一地的旧杂志和旧报纸，还有一个破旧的紫色沙发。墙上贴满了旧海报，这些海报即使在褪了色的情况下，也彰显着夺目的色彩和独特的图案。其中的一张海报上写着：“伟大的盖拉多！”上面是一个戴头巾的人站在流星雨下面。沙发边上紧紧地贴着一个闪闪发光的上了锁的黑色箱子。箱盖上面刻

---

topmost *adj.* 最高的　　snap *v.* 突然折断

glittery *adj.* 闪闪发亮的　　snugly *adv.* 紧密地

the couch. Tiny pictures *carved* into the wood seemed to dance across the lid — ships sailed, horses *trotted*, and stars twinkled.

Miguel looked down at his feet and found an old skeleton key. Its shape and shine had almost worn away, but a golden letter G still beamed through its dullness. Miguel kneeled next to the chest. He cleared *cobwebs* from the keyhole and turned the key in the lock. It clicked!

Benjamin's Bathtub

Miguel lifted the lid to the old chest, hoping to find gold coins, jewels, or swords inside. He *peeked* inside, and his heart sank. The chest was full, not with treasure, but with books.

着栩栩如生的图画——航行的小船，奔跑的骏马和闪烁的星星。

米格尔低头在地上寻找，发现了一把旧的万能钥匙。它已经被磨得几乎看不出原来的形状，也没有了光泽。但是，上面的金色字母G仍然很显眼。米格尔跪在箱子旁边，擦去了钥匙孔里的蜘蛛网。然后将钥匙插到了锁上，锁啪的一声开了！

本杰明的浴缸

米格尔掀开了箱盖，期待着能在里面发现金币、珠宝或是宝剑。他朝箱子里面看了一眼，心里很失望。箱子里面全是书，根本没有珠宝。

---

carve *v.* 雕刻
cobweb *n.* 蜘蛛网
trot *v.* （马等）快跑
peek *v.* 窥视

"Who would keep old books in such a cool trunk?" he asked himself, picking up a thick, black book with fancy lettering: The Story of Benjamin Franklin.

"Ugh," he ***muttered***, "a boring ***biography***." He tried to put the book back, but for some reason he felt he had to open it. He focused on the words, Chapter Eight: Benjamin's Bathtub, when his mom's voice distracted him.

"Miguel, what are you doing?" she called out from the diner's front counter.

"Reading."

"Really?" his mom asked.

"谁会用这么精美的箱子存放旧书呢？"他心里边想边捡起一本厚厚的黑色封皮的书，上面用优美的字体写着："本杰明·富兰克林的故事"。

"哦，"他喃喃地说，"原来是一本无聊的传记。"他试图把书放回去，但不知怎么地，他不由自主地翻开了这本书。他看到上面写着："第八章：本杰明的浴缸"，这时他被妈妈的声音打断了。

"米格尔，你干什么呢？"她在餐厅的前台喊道。

"看书。"

"真的吗？"妈妈问。

---

mutter *v.* 低声嘀咕；嘟囔

biography *n.* 传记

"Yeah, really."

He glanced back down at the words: During the American *Revolution* ... but they became strangely *fuzzy* and danced around on the page.

"asked Benjamin to Franklin France. was to Congress go"

Miguel squeezed his eyes shut. His balance shifted, as if the floor moved beneath him. Salty air stung his eyes and *tingled* his tongue. Miguel no longer smelled the dusty, old loft ...

"I'm an old man of seventy," a man's voice called out, "on a *perilous* journey to France."

"是啊，真的。"

他又接着低下头看书上的字："在美国独立战争期间…… "可是这些字不可思议地变得模糊起来，一个个从书页上飞了出来。

"让本杰明去富兰克林法国。是去国会"

米格尔紧紧地闭上了眼睛。他感到天旋地转，好像地面在他身下移动。咸涩的空气扑面而来，刺痛了他的眼睛和舌头。不再有弥漫着灰尘的破旧阁楼里的气味了。

"我已经年过七旬，"一个男人的声音传来，"却还要冒着危险前往法国。"

---

revolution *n.* 革命

fuzzy *adj.* 模糊的

tingle *v.* 使……感到刺痛

perilous *adj.* 危险的

Miguel opened his eyes to find himself aboard a ship on the ocean, sitting on a wooden lid that covered a... a *bathtub*! One end of the *lid* was open, and out popped an old man's head.

"Temple, my grandson, America shall be free!" The man looked directly at Miguel.

An image of a face on an old half-dollar that he had gotten from his own grandpa flashed before Miguel. This was Benjamin Franklin!

Miguel had been transported into the biography he had flipped open, and now Ben Franklin thought Miguel was his grandson, Temple!

米格尔睁开眼睛，发现自己在海上的一艘船上，坐在一个木盖上，它竟然覆盖着一个……一个浴缸！盖子的另一头是打开的，跃入眼帘的竟然是一个老人的脑袋。

“泰普尔，孙子，美国一定要独立！”老人坚毅地看着米格尔说。

闪现在眼前的这张脸是爷爷给过他的五十美分上的头像。他是本杰明·富兰克林！

米格尔被带到了他翻开的那本自传里，现在本杰明·富兰克林以为米格尔是他的孙子泰普尔！

---

bathtub *n.* 浴缸

lid *n.* 盖子

"Ah, I do wish I were in fair health like you," Ben said. "Then I could make my daily swim at sea. Now I must resort to these baths to *soothe* my aching *joints*."

Miguel tried not to *giggle*—biographies could reveal *intimate* details about a person. Miguel remembered learning that Ben Franklin traveled to France to ask for help in America's fight against the British. He couldn't imagine that Franklin actually brought along a bathtub!

"I have so many questions," Miguel started.

But before he could finish, Ben Franklin's face blurred. Miguel shut his eyes and held his breath. The dusty smell of the loft once again tickled his nose. He was back.

"啊，我真希望自己能拥有跟你一样健康的体魄，"本说，"那样，我就可以每天都在海里游泳了。而现在我却不得不泡在浴缸里，缓解我的关节疼痛。"

米格尔强忍着不让自己笑出来——人物传记总能泄露一个人的隐私。米格尔记得他学到过本杰明·富兰克林在独立战争期间，曾经前往法国求援抗击英国殖民者。他无法想象富兰克林竟然真的带着浴缸！

"我有很多问题，"米格尔开口说。

但没等他说完，本·富兰克林的脸就变得模糊了。米格尔闭上眼睛，屏住呼吸。阁楼的尘土味道又钻进了他的鼻子里。他回来了。

---

soothe *v.* 缓解
joint *n.* 关节
giggle *v.* 咯咯地笑
intimate *adj.* 个人的

Under the Cowboy's Hat

Miguel shut the biography and put it back in the chest. "How could that have happened?" he thought. "Maybe reading biographies isn't so boring after all."

A leather-bound book titled Riding Roundups sat in the row next to the Ben Franklin biography.

"Must be a western," Miguel said, looking at the ***cowboys*** on the cover.

He opened the book and read. Just as Miguel turned the page to Chapter Five: Under the Cowboy's Hat, the words flipped upside down and backward.

戴帽子的牛仔

米格尔合上传记，把它放回箱子。“这是怎么回事？”他想，“也许阅读传记并不那么无聊。”

本·富兰克林传记旁边是一本皮革装订的书，书名是《马背上的围猎》。

“一定是关于西部的故事，”看到封面上的牛仔，米格尔说。

他翻开书，读了起来。就在米格尔翻到“第五章：戴帽子的牛仔”这页的时候，书上的字都反转过来。

---

cowboy *n.* 牛仔

"!lla fo skcirt tsedliw eht wenk dna spudnuor eht edir dluoc xaM yobwoC"

Miguel covered his eyes with his hands. A strong wind that blew against his cheeks brought with it the smell of sweet *sagebrush* and stinky cow *manure*. Miguel was on the prairie, surrounded by a dozen cowboys and hundreds of *longhorn* cattle.

"Lasso those horns!" a cowboy shouted at him from behind.

Arope trembled in Miguel's hands as he realized he'd become a cowboy in the Old West.

Before Miguel could take a breath, the cowboy slipped out his rope, flew past Miguel, *lassoed* the bull's horns, and circled his

---

"！超高艺技且并猎围马骑能斯克马仔牛"

米格尔用手遮住眼睛。一阵强风吹过他的脸颊，风中弥漫着甜蒿夹杂着臭牛粪的味道。米格尔正站在牧场上，周围有十几个牛仔和数百头长角牛。

"快用绳子套住它的角！"一个牛仔在他身后喊道。

意识到自己变成了过去的西部牛仔，米格尔握着绳子的手不停地颤抖着。

还没等米格尔缓过神来，那个牛仔就抛出了他的绳索，绳子从米格尔身旁飞过，套在了那头野牛的两只犄角上，他骑在马上把野牛拴在了树

---

sagebrush *n.* 灌木蒿　　manure *n.* 粪便

longhorn *n.* 长角牛　　lasso *v.* 用套索套捕

stallion around a tree. Miguel stared in ***awe***.

"Cowboy Max," one of the other cowhands shouted, " is still as quick as lightning!"

"Get a move on, Greenie," Cowboy Max said, nodding his head toward Miguel.

Miguel remembered that cowhands in the Old West drove longhorn cattle up trails from Texas to Kansas. Being called a "greenie" must mean that he didn't know what he was doing. "Boy, are they right!" he thought.

Back at camp the smell of coffee and smoked meat hung in the air. Miguel watched the men sitting near the fire playing poker and

---

上。米格尔看得目瞪口呆。

"牛仔马克斯，" 一个牛仔大声喊道，"动作还是那么麻利！"

"让一让，嫩草。" 牛仔马克斯向米格尔点了一下头说。

米格尔记起过去的西部牛仔沿着德克萨斯至堪萨斯的方向，追猎长角牛。叫他"嫩草"，一定是觉得他什么都不懂。"天啊，不能让他们看扁！" 米格尔想。

回到营地，空气中飘着咖啡和熏肉的香味。米格尔看到一些人坐在炉火旁打着扑克，讲着故事。牛仔马克斯摘掉了黑帽子，露出了绑着红色丝

---

awe *n.* 惊叹

telling stories. Cowboy Max removed his black hat and out fell a long gray *braid* tied with a red *ribbon*.

Miguel's mouth dropped. Cowboy Max was a lady!

She smiled at Miguel. "Sorry, Greenie, thought you knew."

He shook his head. "They call you Cowboy Max."

"It's short for Maxine," she said. "Some people don't like women who wear *breeches* and speak up for themselves."

"You still ride?"

"You bet," said Maxine. "I'm my happiest when I'm with my herd."

"You're brave," said Miguel.

带的长长的灰色发辫。

米格尔大吃一惊。牛仔马克斯竟然是女的！

她笑着对米格尔说："怎么了，嫩草，我还以为你知道呢。"

他摇摇头。"他们都叫你牛仔马克斯。"

"那是马克斯辛妮的简称，"她说，"一些人不喜欢女性穿马裤，独立自主。"

"你还会继续骑马吗？"

"当然，"马克斯辛妮说，"跟牛在一起，我才最开心。"

"你真英勇，"米格尔说。

---

braid *n.* 发辫　　ribbon *n.* 丝带

breeches *n.* 马裤

"Just lucky," she said. "I get treated fairly in these parts. A lot of women *ranchers* don't."

Miguel had many questions, but the stars began to blur. He felt dizzy, so he shut his eyes. In an instant, Miguel found himself back at the loft.

The Creature from Copernicus Crater

Miguel sat down on the floor. Life was tough on the prairie, especially for women. He never imagined westerns were so interesting! It was getting late, but Miguel had to try one more book.

A small book with a silver moon on the cover called The Creature from Copernicus *Crater* grabbed his attention.

"我很幸运，"她说，"在这里，我得到了公平的对待。许多女性牛仔都没有这样的好运气。"

米格尔有很多问题，但是天上的星星开始模糊。他感到头晕目眩，所以他闭上眼睛。转瞬之间，米格尔发现自己回到了阁楼。

哥白尼陨石坑的生物

米格尔坐在地板上想着。牧场的生活很艰苦，尤其对于女人更是如此。他从来没有想到过西部这么有趣！天色将晚，但米格尔还想再看一本书。

他的视线被一本封面上印着一轮明月的小书吸引了。书名为《哥白尼

---

rancher *n.* 牧场工人

crater *n.* 陨石坑

"Science fiction?" he thought. "That's weird, the first chapter starts on page 214."

Miguel began to read, "Colonel Chan *guarded* the underground lunar outpost. He hadn't seen another living thing for two years until ..." Suddenly the words streamed together.

"adangerousandmysteriouscreatureappearednearthecrater!"

Miguel *shivered* and closed his eyes. The air seeping into his nostrils smelled artificial, like at a hospital. Computers beeped in the distance. Miguel opened his eyes to find himself in an underground laboratory. Countertops were jammed with high-tech equipment—cameras, *scanners*, and other strange *contraptions*. Jars full of rocks,

---

陨石坑的生物》。

“是科幻小说吗？”他心想，“真奇怪，第一章是从214页开始的。”

米格尔开始读，“陈上校守卫在地下的月球前哨基地。他已经有两年没看到其他的生物了，直到……”突然，所有的字都挤在了一起。

“陨石坑附近发现了危险神秘的生物！”

米格尔颤抖着闭上了眼睛，鼻子里呼吸的空气有点像医院里的味道。远处的计算机在运行着。米格尔睁开眼睛，发现自己在一个地下实验室里。实验台上堆满了高科技的设备——照相机、扫描仪和其他奇怪的玩意儿。架子上装满了各种各样的瓶子，里面装着岩石、灰尘和液体。米格尔

---

guard *v.* 看守

shiver *v.* 颤抖

scanner *n.* 扫描仪

contraption *n.* 奇特的装置

dust, and liquids filled the shelves. Miguel picked up a jar and read: Copernicus Crater Lunar Rocks.

"Lunar rocks?" Miguel whispered. "I'm on the moon!"

Miguel raced out the lab's door and through long, silent *corridors*, hoping to find a view of the moon. He followed the red lights that dotted the floor. He pushed open a door that read "Exit Room". Something *beeped* in the pocket of his *jumpsuit*. Miguel pulled out a radio *communicator*.

"Colonel Chan?" a woman said. "This is Mission Control."

Miguel pressed the red button and tried to sound official. "This is Colonel Chan."

拿起一个瓶子，看到上面写着："哥白尼陨石坑的月球岩石"。

"月球岩石？"米格尔低声说。"我在月球！"

米格尔跑出实验室，穿过一条长长的寂静的走廊，希望能看到月球上的景色。他沿着地板上镶嵌着的红灯走，推开了一扇写着"出口"的门。他工作服的口袋里有东西在响，米格尔掏出了一个无线电通信器。

"陈上校吗？"一个女人说。"我是总控室。"

米格尔按下红色按钮，学着军官的口吻说："我是陈上校。"

---

corridor *n.* 走廊
beep *v.* 嘟嘟响
jumpsuit *n.* 连衣裤
communicator *n.* 通信器

"This is Colonel Lundy," she said. "We need you to get outside now and *investigate* some strange activity near the crater."

Miguel *gulped*. Being on the moon alone would be terrifying!

"Get out there now, and report back what you find." Colonel Lundy said.

I can do it, he told himself as he tried to figure out how to work the spacesuit. After all, I'm an *astronaut* now.

He put on his *helmet*, engaged the door, and stepped out onto the moon...

The sky was deep black. Miguel stepped forward and hopped into the air. Lunar gravity made him as light as a feather! "I must weigh less than twenty pounds!" he thought.

"我是伦迪上校，"她说，"我们需要你现在到外面，查看一下陨石坑附近的奇怪现象。"

米格尔倒抽了一口气。一个人待在月球上会很吓人！

"马上去那儿，并汇报你的发现。" 伦迪上校说。

"我能做到的。"他对自己说。同时，他想弄清怎么穿航天服。"不管怎么说，我现在是宇航员了。"

他戴上自己的头盔，打开舱门，踏上了月球的土地……

天色黑暗。米格尔迈开双腿，在太空漫步。月球的重力使他轻如羽毛！他想："我现在肯定少于20磅！"

---

investigate *v.* 调查

gulp *v.* 大口地吸气

astronaut *n.* 宇航员

helmet *n.* 头盔

He leaped and jumped across the silvery gray hills, leaving boot marks in the dust. He looked up and stopped dead in his tracks. There in the sky hung a crescent-shaped Earth!

Then Miguel sensed a dark shape moving toward him. He turned, and something struck him from behind, sending him sailing through the air like a ***helium*** balloon that had been cut free. He couldn't stop! Miguel floated past a tower, clung to the side, and ***shimmied*** down to the ground. There, Miguel came face to face with the ugliest creature he'd ever seen!

Bulging, laser-like eyes ***glowed*** from the fleshy face of a creature almost as white as the moon. Miguel threw his body forward, hop-skipping out of there as fast as he could. Red laser eye-shots

---

他跳过了一座座银灰色的小山包，在尘土上留下了足迹。他抬头向上望，停住了脚步。天空中挂着一个新月形的地球！

米格尔感觉到一个黑影在向着他的方向移动。他转过身，不知什么东西从后面打了他一下，他被打得飘到了空中，就好像放飞了的氦气球，根本停不下来！米格尔飘过一座塔，用手抓住了塔边，顺着塔边向下爬到了地面。然后，米格尔见到了世界上最丑陋的生物。

一张模糊的惨白的脸上，一对向前凸起激光一样的眼睛闪闪发光。米格尔抻着脖子，拼命地奔跑跳跃。红色的激光眼射出的激光在米格尔身旁呼啸而过。他慌张地扑向月球前哨。

---

helium *n.* 氦

shimmy *v.* 摇动

glow *v.* 发光

whizzed passed Miguel. He lunged for the lunar outpost in a panic.

His breath fogged his visor. He tripped on a rock and *tumbled* forward, doing a complete *somersault* in the air. The creature groaned, its *gooey* arms almost upon him.

Miguel tapped all the buttons on the door panel, finally opening the door. He slipped through just in time! As Miguel *stumbled* in, he accidentally activated his radio communicator.

"Mission Control."

"Something tried to kill me!" Miguel gasped.

But before anyone could answer, the Exit Room walls blurred. Miguel closed his eyes and was happy to feel the soft, warm couch beneath him.

他呼出的空气在面罩里形成了雾气。他绊在了一个石头上，向前跌倒了，结结实实地摔在了地上。那个怪物抱怨着，它黏糊糊的爪子差一点就抓住他了。

米格尔把门上所有按钮都拍了一遍，总算打开了门。他刚好及时跳了进去。就在他跌倒的瞬间，无意中启动了他的无线电通信器。

“总控室。”

“有个东西想杀我！”米格尔喘着气说。

还没听到回答，出口处的门就变得模糊起来。米格尔闭上眼睛，当他感觉自己坐在了柔软温暖的沙发上时，很高兴。

---

tumble *v.* 跌倒

somersault *n.* 跟头

gooey *adj.* 黏的

stumble *v.* 绊脚

Great-Grandpa George

Miguel *slumped* over onto the chest. "Science fiction was terrifying and *thrilling* all at the same time!" he thought.

The shop would be closed soon, and Miguel knew that after his mom locked the doors, she would ask to see his essay. He put the books back, leaving the key in the lock.

When he got down from the loft, Miguel picked up his pencil. It felt good in his hand. Ideas were fresh in his mind, so Miguel's words flowed easily, like pouring *syrup* on *pancakes*.

Miguel finished his outline and read it to his mom.

"Not bad for someone who thinks reading is boring," she said.

曾祖父乔治

米格尔倒在了箱子上。"科幻小说可真是令人毛骨悚然啊！"他想。

汉堡店很快就要关门了，米格尔知道，妈妈锁上门后就会来检查他写的作文。他把书放回原处，用钥匙锁上了箱子。

从阁楼下来后，米格尔捡起铅笔。手中握着笔，米格尔感到思路很清晰，语言很流畅，文思如泉涌。

米格尔写完了提纲读给妈妈听。

"认为阅读无聊的人能写成这样已经很不错了，"她说。

---

slump *v.* 倒下

thrilling *adj.* 毛骨悚然的

syrup *n.* 糖浆

pancake *n.* 烙饼

"I found some stuff up in the loft back there..."

"Your great-grandpa's stuff?" his mom said.

"Great-Grandpa George?"

"Yes, he was a ***magician*** called the Great Gallardo!"

"Really?"

"He performed all over the world," she said. "And he ran his magic shop right here."

"Why didn't you tell me?"

"Maybe I was waiting for the right time." Miguel's mom ***winked***. "You know the most magical thing about him?"

"我在后面的阁楼发现了一些东西……"

"你曾祖父的东西吗？"他妈妈说。

"曾祖父乔治？"

"是的，他是一个魔法师，被称为伟大的盖拉多！"

"真的吗？"

"他在世界各地巡演，"她说，"他经营的魔法商店就在这里。"

"你为什么没告诉过我呢？"

"也许我在等待合适的时机。"米格尔的妈妈向他眨了眨眼睛说："你知道他最神奇的是什么吗？"

---

magician *n.* 魔法师

wink *v.* 眨眼

Miguel's heart *raced*. "What?"

"He loved to read more than anything else."

Miguel smiled.

His mom smiled back.

Thanks to The Great Gallardo's books, maybe Miguel did too. He couldn't wait to find more adventures in the glittery black chest in the loft.

米格尔的心跳得很厉害。“什么？”

“他对书籍的热爱远远超过对其他事物的喜爱。”

米格尔笑了。

妈妈也笑了。

感谢伟大的盖拉多的那些书，也许也是米格尔的书。他迫不及待地想在阁楼的闪闪发光的箱子里，找到更多的探险故事。

---

race *v.* 急速跳动，快速转动

4

Fast Forward to the Future

All Play and No Work

"Score!" Miguel Ventura's fingers flew over his video controller. He *zapped* swarms of alien crabmonsters that cruised the beach on his TV. "I just beat the game!"

"Ya-hoo!" his friend Trevon yelled. They *slapped* a high-five.

飞向未来

只玩不干活

“得分了！”米格尔·文图拉的手指飞快地按动着游戏手柄。他在攻击电视上的外星螃蟹怪物，它们一拨接着一拨地从海岸上涌过来。“我刚刚过关了！”

“太棒了！”他的朋友特莱文欢呼着说。他们击了一下手掌。

“该干活了吧，”米格尔的妹妹特丽莎说着拿出了一张单子。“先洗盘子，然后洗衣服，吸尘，还有掸灰。”

---

zap *v.* 攻击　　　slap *v.* 击掌

"Time to get to work," said Miguel's sister, Teresa, as she checked her list. "Dishes first, then laundry, *vacuuming*, and dusting."

"Sorry, sis. "The boys laughed.

"We only finished the first game."

"Nine more to go!" Trevon added.

Teresa planted herself in front of the TV screen. "Mom and Dad said we could only stay home if we did our chores."

The Ventura family owned a sandwich shop, which is where Miguel and Teresa often spent their afternoons and weekends helping out.

"You've got a handle on it, Tee." Miguel *slid* her aside.

"抱歉，老妹。" 两个男孩笑了起来。

"我们只是过了第一关。"

"还有九关没过呢！" 特莱文补充道。

特丽莎挡在了电视屏幕前。"爸妈说我们只有干家务活才能待在家里。"

文图拉一家经营着一家三明治店，米格尔和特丽莎经常在下午和周末去那里帮忙。

"你来处理这个，特丽莎。" 米格尔把她推开。

---

vacuum *v.* 吸尘

slid *v.* （使）快捷而悄声地移动

"Fine!" Teresa *tossed* her list at Miguel. "You'll get grounded, not me."

Trevon *shoved* chips into his mouth. *Crumbs* cascaded down his chin like a waterfall.

Miguel flopped onto the *cushions* of the couch. "This is the life!"

Vrrroooom! Teresa revved the vacuum in front of the TV.

"Move!" Miguel yelled.

Teresa shrugged.

She flipped off the switch.

"You two are slugs!" She yanked the cord. "Wasting your life away."

"够了！"特丽莎在米格尔眼前晃动着那张单子。"你来搞定这些，我不管。"

特莱文往嘴里塞着薯片。屑沫像瀑布一样从他的下巴不断地往下落。

米格尔揮揮沙发上的坐垫。"这才是生活！"

嗡嗡！特丽莎在电视前面开始吸尘。

"躲开！"米格尔大喊。

特丽莎耸了耸肩。

她一下子关掉了开关。

"你们两个懒汉！"她收起了电线说。"你们在浪费生命。"

---

toss *v.* 扔

shove *v.* 乱塞

crumb *n.* 碎屑

cushion *n.* 垫子

"If this is the life of a *slug*…" Trevon said.

"... we'll take it." Miguel answered. "We've got all the time in the world."

Five minutes later, the phone rang. "It's for you, Trevon!" Teresa called out.

"Hello?" Trevon *mumbled* into the phone. "Why?" He shrugged. "Fine. Be home in a minute."

"What's up?" Miguel asked.

"Mom says I have to go," he said

"What did you do, Tee?" Miguel rushed through the house.

"如果懒汉的生活是这样的……"特莱文说。

"……那我们宁愿做懒汉。"米格尔接着说。"我们就成天玩。"

五分钟后，电话铃响了。"特莱文，找你的。"特丽莎喊道。

"你好？"特莱文在电话里小声地嘀咕着。"为什么？"他耸了一下肩说："好的，我马上就回家。"

"什么事？"米格尔问。

"妈妈说我得走了，"他说。

"你都做了什么，特丽莎？"米格尔冲进房里说。

---

slug *n.* 懒汉　　mumble *v.* 嘀咕

Silence.

"I'll show her," Miguel muttered under his breath as he slipped out the door, heading directly for the sandwich shop. "Even without Trevon, there'll be no chores for me."

Miguel had found the Great Gallardo's books last year in an old chest up in the loft of his parents' shop. The books belonged to his great-grandpa, a magician called the Great Gallardo. Somehow, Miguel was able to travel into the stories and become a ***character***. Getting lost in the center of the Earth was the scariest thing he had done. Becoming the ***Scarecrow*** from *The Wizard of Oz* had been the most fun.

没有人回答。

“我要让她看看，”米格尔从家里走了出来，径直朝三明治店走去。他小声地嘟囔着：“即使没有特莱文，我也不会做家务。”

米格尔去年在父母店里的阁楼上发现了伟大的盖拉多的书，它们放在一个旧箱子里。这些书是曾祖父盖拉多的，他是一个魔法师。不知怎么地，米格尔能进到书里，变成书中的人物。其中最恐怖的经历就是他在地球的中心迷了路。最有趣的旅程就是变成了绿野仙踪中的稻草人。

---

character *n.* 人物，角色　　scarecrow *n.* 稻草人

Dust covered the chest of books. An old *wrench* stuck out from the lid. Miguel slipped it into his pocket, knowing that he'd need it on his journey. Even after so many trips, he didn't have a *clue* how the magic worked. Miguel pulled out a small blue book. "The Time Machine by H.G. Wells," he said. "Cool, I get to go to the future!"

He started reading from page 326. "I heard nothing but the cracking of *twigs* under my feet, my own breathing, and the throb of my blood *vessels* in my ears." The words danced across the page and Miguel's heart quickened its beat. "then some underworld Morlocks voices there caught I had heard and several they sounds in I closing and me the on the in and were ..."

箱子上蒙着厚厚的一层灰。一个旧扳子卡在了箱盖里，米格尔顺手把它放在了口袋里，他知道在旅行中会用到它。即使穿越了这么多次，他仍然不明白一切是怎么发生的。米格尔抽出了一本蓝色的小书。“《时间机器》，作者：威尔。”他念着。“太酷了，我要去未来世界了！”

他翻到了326页。“除了脚踩在树枝上的声音，我自己的呼吸声还有耳朵里血管跳动的声音，我什么都听不到。”这些字飞过书页，米格尔的心跳得很厉害。“然后一些来自地下的莫洛克人 声音 抓 我听过的……”

---

wrench *n.* 扳手　　clue *n.* 线索

twig *n.* 树枝　　vessel *n.* 血管

Miguel's view *blurred*. His head whirled. Light coming through the window zipped in and out. Miguel spun faster and faster. Light and dark transformed into gray.

Was this time traveling? Miguel's body grew heavy and suddenly flung forward, *slamming* to the ground. Then all went dark.

Humanity Lost

Miguel found himself lying in a forest clearing at the base of a hill. A small girl lay curled up behind him. Curly hair *adorned* with flowers framed her face, which had *delicate* features. Who was she?

A fire hissed from across the clearing. Flickering beams of light from the fire danced across the girl's dress. Flames sprang up from

---

米格尔的视线开始模糊了。他的头晕晕的。从窗子外面照进来的光忽明忽暗。米格尔越转越快。眼前的白色和黑色混合成了灰色。

这就是时间旅程吗？米格尔的身体越来越重了，突然猛冲下来，砰的一声摔在了地上。接着，眼前一片漆黑。

消失的文明

米格尔发现自己正躺在林中的一片空地上，就在山脚下。一个小女孩躺在他身后。卷头发再配上带着花环的脸，真是个漂亮的人。她是谁呢？

空地上燃烧着的火发出嘶嘶的声音。星星点点的火苗蹿到了女孩的衣服上。火势蔓延得很快。一块木板上的火星点着了附近的树木和树丛，速

---

blur *v.* 模糊

slam *v.* 猛劲一摔

adorn *v.* 装饰

delicate *adj.* 娇美的

a pile of wood to catch nearby trees and bushes on fire and traveled through the forest like a pack of lions. Miguel *panicked*. As he jumped to his feet, he kicked an iron bar on the ground. Voices mumbled in the darkness beyond the firelight. Bushes rustled. Footsteps padded the ground. Miguel turned round and round. Someone was coming. Something was coming.

The flames exposed several white creatures with *gorilla*-like faces rushing toward him. Standing upright, they were about the same size as Miguel. Suddenly he remembered the story. These things were called Morlocks, ape-like *beasts* that lived underground...and they were *cannibals*!

度惊人。米格尔很慌张。站起来时，他踢到了一根铁棍。一片黑暗中，火光那边传来了一个模糊的声音。树枝沙沙作响，脚步踏在地上发出阵阵的声响。米格尔来回踱着步。有人来了，会有事情发生。

通过火焰的光亮，米格尔看到了几个长得像大猩猩一样的白色生物，它们正向他跑过来。如果站直的话，这些生物大约跟米格尔一样高。突然他记起了那个故事。这些生物是莫洛克人，它们长得像猿猴，生活在地下……还有他们是食人族。

---

panicked *v.* 恐慌
beast *n.* 野兽
gorilla *n.* 大猩猩
cannibal *n.* 食人族

Miguel gulped. The Morlocks nearly surrounded him.

"Wake up, little girl." He shook her, keeping one eye on the Morlocks.

Her big blue eyes opened. "I'm Weena."

"That means I'm the time traveler!" He picked her up. "And we're dinner for those Morlocks!"

Weena jumped out of his arms and *sprinted* into the forest, which grew brighter and hotter from the *inferno*. Miguel reached out, but she slipped away. For a moment, Weena stopped in front of the blaze, *mesmerized* by the dancing flames. Then she moved forward.

"No, fire!" He motioned toward the heat. "Ouch!"

米格尔吓了一跳。莫洛克人已经把他包围了。

“醒醒，小姑娘。”他摇晃着她，还要盯着莫洛克人。

那双蓝色的大眼睛睁开了。“我叫维拉。”

“那我就是时空旅行者！”他拉起女孩说，“我们就要成为这些莫洛克人的晚餐了!”

维拉从他怀里挣脱出去，向森林冲去。此时，整个森林火光冲天。米格尔想要抓住她，但她挣脱了。维拉在熊熊燃烧的烈火前站了一会儿，被飞舞着的火苗蛊惑了。然后，她向火中走去。

“不要，小心火！”他向热浪接近。“噢！”

---

sprint *v.* 冲刺　　inferno *n.* 大火灾

mesmerize *v.* 迷惑

Weena had no clue what he was saying. From the story, Miguel knew that 80,000 years into the future, human beings had changed, and split into two groups. Weena was an Eloi, the people who lived aboveground. Over time, their easy life had made them weaker and less intelligent than the Morlocks, who were the ***primitive*** worker-class who lived underground and built machinery. The Morlocks only came aboveground at night to hunt the Eloi.

Miguel shivered. Smoke burned his nostrils. Weena stumbled back to where they started and ***collapsed***. He tried to wake her, but he could ***barely*** tell whether she was breathing. From behind, Miguel felt fingers ***cling*** to his back. They gripped his neck. Arms.

维拉根本没听见他的话。从这个故事里，米格尔了解到未来八万年的样子，人类的物种发生了变化，演变为两个种群。维拉是个埃洛伊人，他们生活在地面上。长时间的安逸生活使他们变得远远没有莫洛克人强壮和聪明。那些莫洛克人原来是工人阶层，生活在地下，制造机器。莫洛克人只在晚上来到地面上，猎食埃洛伊人。

米格尔浑身发抖。炽热的浓烟熏进了他的鼻腔。维拉跌跌撞撞地回到了他们相遇的地方，跌倒了。米格尔试图唤醒她，可他不敢确定她是否还有呼吸。米格尔感到身后有人用手指抓住了他的后背。抓住了他的脖子还有手臂。他四处张望了一下，弯下腰，抓起了地面上的一根铁棍。

---

primitive *adj.* 原来的

collapse *v.* 跌倒

barely *adv.* 几乎不

cling *v.* 抓紧；紧抱

He *swiveled* around, bent down, and grabbed the iron bar off the ground.

"I'm not your dinner!" He lunged toward the Morlocks, waving the bar in the air. "Get away from us!" The Morlocks scattered.

He turned back. Weena had disappeared! His heart fell; he hadn't protected her.

Another Morlock tugged at his ankle.

Miguel kicked his foot out and *scrambled* up the hill.

A Beautiful Machine

From the hilltop, the glow of the fire *illuminated* the entire forest. Ashes and *embers* glittered the ground, burning Miguel's feet. He

---

"别吃我！"他向那些莫洛克人刺去，在空中挥舞着铁棍。"别碰我们！"莫洛克人吓得向后闪了一下。

他转过身来。维拉不见了！他心里一沉，他没能保护好她。

又来了一个莫洛克人用力拉他的脚踝。

米格尔使劲踢了一脚，向山上爬去。

美丽的机器

从山顶上往下看，火光把整个森林照得通亮。地上落着没燃尽的灰烬，烤着米格尔的双脚。米格尔用大绿叶包在脚的周围。

---

swivel *v.* 转身
illuminate *v.* 照亮
scramble *v.* 爬
ember *n.* 余烬

wrapped huge green leaves around them.

A group of trees exploded like *dynamite*, sending Miguel to the ground. The ape-like creatures froze near the edge of the blaze. The fire singed their white hair, creating a *putrid* stench. They fell like *dominoes*, succumbing to the hungry beast of a fire. They, like Weena, had never seen a blaze like this. The future was nothing as Miguel imagined.

The surviving Morlocks streamed through the trees, the fire *chasing* them like a monster. Miguel followed them. Maybe they would lead him back to the time machine, and he could get home.

Miguel hustled past trees as tall as buildings and brushed against

---

一片大树突然倒地，把米格尔砸到了。那些猿一样的生物站在火焰的边上。火燎着了他们的白头发，散发出恶臭。他们像多米诺骨牌一样倒下，被肆虐的大火烧死了。跟维拉一样，他们从来没见过这么大的火。米格尔感到未来不像自己想象的那么好。

幸存下来的莫洛克人涌进森林，大火像猛兽一样追赶着他们。米格尔跟在他们身后，也许他们会把自己带回到时间机器那儿，那样他就能回家了。

米格尔穿梭在跟楼一样高的树林中，树枝上的蓝色花朵跟他的脸一样

---

dynamite *n.* 炸药

domino *n.* 多米诺骨牌

putrid *adj.* 腐臭的

chase *v.* 追赶

blue flowers as big as his face. There was no technology in the future, and Miguel *surmised* that was the reason why nature *flourished*. The Morlocks disappeared into an underground passageway, leaving Miguel alone near a marble statue of a *sphinx*.

The shiny valves around the sphinx's bronze base shimmered in the firelight. In the story, the Morlocks unscrewed the valves to open this statue so they could capture the time traveler inside it. Miguel was too close behind them for the Morlocks to set the trap this time. Miguel had figured it out—the time machine was inside!

Miguel pulled on the *valves*. Twisted.Tugged. They slipped through his fingers. Dread spread over him like a storm cloud. How would he

---

大。未来世界里没有科技，米格尔想这就是为什么大自然如此昌盛。那些莫洛克人钻进了一条地下通道，不见了，把米格尔独自留在了一座大理石的狮身人面像旁边。

狮身人面像的铜座上的阀门在火光的映照下闪闪发光。在故事中，莫洛克人拧开了阀门，打开了雕像，捕获了里面的时光穿梭者。米格尔在他们身后跟得很近，莫洛克人现在没有办法给他设陷阱。米格尔已经明白了，时间机器就在里面！

米格尔使劲拉着阀门。用手拧，用手拖。它们在他的手中纹丝不动。恐惧向阴云一样，笼罩着他，他怎么才能登上时光机器呢?

---

surmise *v.* 猜测

flourish *v.* 昌盛

sphinx *n.* 狮身人面

valve *n.* 阀门

get to the machine?

Miguel thought of Weena. Then he thought of Teresa and how he'd been mad at her when he left. What if he never made it back? Miguel leaned against the statue. Something from his pocket *clanked* against the bronze. The wrench from the loft!

He ripped the tool from his pocket and fit it onto the valves. Perfect! He *torqued* them hard. The front panel of the statue came loose, slid down into the ground, and *revealed* the time machine!

Miguel rushed over. It was beautiful; a cross between a race car and the gears of a fancy watch. The *rectangular* metal frame supported twisted crystal and ivory bars that interconnected,

---

米格尔想到了维拉。然后想到了特丽莎和他离开时对她恶劣的态度。如果他再也回不去了可怎么办？米格尔靠在雕像上。他的口袋里好像有什么东西咣当的一声撞在了铜像上。是阁楼里带来的扳手！

他从口袋里掏出工具，放在阀门上试了一下。刚好合适！他使劲地拧着阀门。铜像前面的挡板松动了，落到了地上，一架时光机露了出来！

米格尔跑过去。它很漂亮，像是跑车和名表里的齿轮的结合体。长方形的金属框架支撑着互相交织的螺旋形的水晶和象牙做成的栏杆，一直向上延伸。它看起来像是一道花很长时间也解不开的智力难题。

---

clank *v.* 发出当啷声
torque *v.* 拧
reveal *v.* 使显露
rectangular *adj.* 长方形的

creating one, *continuous* pattern. It was like the *ultimate* brain puzzle, the kind you could work on for hours yet never solve.

But to Miguel, the idea of time travel was the biggest puzzle. He knew it was impossible in the real world, but he fantasized about moving through space and time: the fourth dimension.

The front panel inside held two levers and three dials labeled with the numbers up to a million. The levers would take him forward and back. The *dials* would show how many days he'd traveled. How would he know which one to push?

The bronze panel of the statue shot up and clanked shut. He was trapped in the dark! His hands *fumbled* for the levers. He heard

---

但是，现在对米格尔来说，最大的难题是怎么穿越时光。他知道这在现实世界里是不可能的，但是他还是很迷恋穿越时空：到第四度空间去。

时光机的前面有两个操纵杆，三个表盘，能表示从一到一百万的数字。这个表盘就是用来表示他能穿越的时间的，他怎么才能知道应该推动哪根操纵杆呢?

雕像的铜质前挡板啪的一声合上了。他被困在了黑暗中！他用手试探着，想要摸到操纵杆。他听到了嘀嘀咕咕的声音和脚步声，还有笑声。这

---

continuous *adj.* 持续的　　ultimate *adj.* 最高的

dial *n.* 表盘　　fumble *v.* 摸索

murmurs. Footsteps. Laughter. Miguel was not alone. Warm bodies pressed near him. They pulled on his clothes. *Tugged* at his feet. Grabbed his shoulders.

He backed against the panel, kicking, screaming, and flailing his arms, surrounded by the Morlocks' *musty* smell, their steaming breath, their fury. Miguel fumbled in his pockets. He pulled out the wrench and waved it. One of the Morlocks knocked it away.

He felt the prick of teeth against his neck. Miguel *lunged* forward, knocking his head into the closest Morlock for the ultimate head-butt! In that same instant, he reached out for the levers. The

---

里不是米格尔一个人。一个个热乎乎的身体向他逼近。他们撕扯着他的衣服，拖拽着他的脚，抓挠着他的肩膀。

他靠在时光机的挡板上，踢着脚、尖叫着、挥舞着手臂。周围都是莫洛克人发霉的气味，热乎乎的呼吸，还有他们的愤怒。米格尔把手伸进口袋。掏出扳手，疯狂地挥舞着。一个莫洛克人打掉了他的扳手。

他感到有牙齿咬住了他的脖子。米格尔向前冲去，狠狠地用头把离他最近的一个莫洛克人撞倒在地！同时，伸手够到了操纵杆。米格尔的手指

---

murmur *n.* 低语；喃喃声
tug *v.* 用力拖
musty *adj.* 发霉的
lunge *v.* 突然前冲

Morlocks tumbled out of the machine as Miguel's fingers clamped down onto metal. He pulled hard.

Blackness disappeared. Gray haze. Whirling thoughts. The dials spun wildly, like the second hand on a clock. All at once, Miguel's body *surged* forward. Everything stopped.

He'd gone forward. Fast forward.

Dying to See the Future

Miguel found himself thrust upon a black, endless *plateau* scattered with black bushes. The land was flat with no mountains, hills, rivers, or oceans. The sun hung in the gray sky. The *fiery* star

---

扳动那个金属杆的一刹那，那些莫洛克人跌出了时光机。他又使劲地拉了一下。

黑暗消失了，出现了一道灰光。天旋地转。表盘开始疯狂地旋转，好像时钟上的秒针。顷刻间，米格尔的身体向前一冲，一切都停止了。

他到了未来，非常远的未来。

梦寐以求的未来

米格尔发现自己被抛到了一个黑漆漆的，无边无际的高原上。上面稀稀落落地长着几棵树。这块土地很平坦，没有高山，丘陵，河流或是海洋。太阳挂在灰蒙蒙的天空中。这个曾经炽热红彤彤的恒星现在变成了橙

---

surge *v.* 猛冲
plateau *n.* 高原
fiery *adj.* 炽热的

was now orange, and its rays pulsed as if it were losing power.

From across the plain, a long creature *crawled* toward Miguel on thousands of feet. It rose thirty feet high and had *overlapping* greenish-black plates covering its body. Multiple black eyes stared him down. As it got closer, two horn-like *antennas* stretched out like hands. It was a giant *centipede*, and it was coming after him!

Miguel scrambled back into the machine. He tugged on a lever. Instantly, the sky grew darker. He whirled forward, but the alternating of day and night-sunrise and sunset-slowed. The dials spun forward again and again. The time machine stopped abruptly.

色，无力地散发着微弱的光芒。

在平原上，一只长长的大虫子向米格尔爬过来，它的脚足足有好几千只。它大概有30英尺长，全身上下覆盖着深绿色的硬壳。黑色的复眼向下盯着米格尔。走到米格尔近旁时，伸出两只跟牛角一样大的触角。它是一只巨大的蜈蚣，就在他身后！

米格尔爬进时光机里。他拖动了一下其中的一个操纵杆。天空转瞬之间变黑了。他又向前转了一下操纵杆，日夜交替，日升日落，然后渐渐地慢了下来。表盘一圈一圈地向前转。突然，时光机停了下来。

---

crawl *v.* 爬行

antenna *n.* 触角

overlapping *adj.* 重叠的

centipede *n.* 蜈蚣

The sun, now red and large, hung along the *horizon*. The sky was an *inky* black, missing its moon, and highlighted by only a few pale stars. Like the scarlet of the sun, reddish rocks lined the beach where Miguel stood. Strange *fluorescent* green plants seemed to be the only thing growing.

The ocean was still—no waves, no breakers, no wind. Miguel sat down. It was hard to breathe. He remembered the same feeling when he'd hiked up Mount Whitney, the tallest mountain in California, with his mom. Oxygen was scarce.

The bitter cold *nipped* at his fingers as he cruised over the rocky

太阳现在又红又大地挂在地平线上。天空呈现出一片漆黑的颜色，看不到月亮，只有几颗暗淡的小星星点缀在它的周围。像太阳一样猩红的岩石林立在米格尔脚下的海岸上。那些散发着奇怪荧光的绿色植物好像是唯一发光的物体。

海面很平静，没有大浪、微波，也没有风。米格尔坐下来。感到呼吸困难。他想起了自己跟妈妈爬上惠特尼山顶时，也是同样的感觉，惠特尼山是加利福尼亚最高的山峰。那里缺少氧气。

他在岩石林立的海滩游荡的时候，一阵阵刺骨的寒冷咬啮着他的指

horizon *n.* 地平线　　inky *adj.* 漆黑的

fluorescent *adj.* 荧光的　　nip *v.* 咬住

beach. The red ball in the sky was a sad picture of what the sun used to be. Was he witnessing the death of the sun and the end of life on Earth? He *swallowed*. Such a huge question was hard to *comprehend*. A gust of fear and sadness brushed across him. He had to get home. But how?

From the *craggy* shore, Miguel stepped down onto a boulder. It moved under his feet!

He jumped back when a huge claw reared up from the ground. It was a crab-like creature as big as a table! Its huge antennas swung like *whips* right at Miguel.

尖。天空中的太阳已经失去了往日的雄风。他看到的不会是太阳的毁灭，地球的末日吧？他咽了一口吐沫。这么大的问题他理解不了。他感到一阵恐惧和哀伤。他得回家。可是怎么才能回去呢？

从崎岖的海岸下来，米格尔跳到了一块光滑的石头上。可是它竟然在米格尔的脚下移动！

他赶紧跳了回去，一个巨大的钳子从地面上升起来。是一只跟桌子一样大的像螃蟹一样的动物！它巨大的触角像鞭子一样抽打在了米格尔的身上。

---

swallow *v.* 吞咽

comprehend *v.* 充分了解

craggy *adj.* 崎岖的

whip *n.* 鞭子

As he scrambled backward, Miguel tripped, slamming into the rocky shore.

The crab moved forward, its huge claws grasping, its eyes *gleaming* toward its next meal.

Miguel ran. As he turned back, the crab opened its mouth and lunged toward Miguel. Antennas swept over the back of Miguel's neck. His foot caught between two rocks. He tugged. *Jerked*. Kicked. He was stuck!

The crab came closer.

Miguel *squirmed*.

米格尔在向后退的时候，跌倒了，摔在了崎岖的海岸上。

那只螃蟹向前挪动着，舞动着爪子，眼睛贪婪地看着它的美味。

米格尔跑了起来。他回头看见那只螃蟹张着嘴，向他扑过来。触角刚好触到米格尔的脖子。他的脚卡在了两个岩石中间。他又拖又拽又踢。他被卡住了！

那只螃蟹离得很近了。

米格尔不停地扭动着身体。

---

gleam *v.* 发光

jerk *v.* 急拉；猛推

squirm *v.* 扭动

Closer.

Miguel yelled.

Closer.

Miguel grabbed small rocks off the ground and began to throw. He picked up one after another, left hand, right hand, *tossing* them as quick as he could. The creature *flinched*. Miguel bounced more rocks against its hard shell. The crab slowed.

It was working!

Left. Right. Left. Right. He pictured himself in front of his TV, *blasting* the alien crabs from his video game. But this time, it was all too real! With one last heave, Miguel sent a basketball-sized rock

---

越来越近了。

米格尔大声叫喊。

更近了。

米格尔从地上抓起一些小石头，朝它扔去。他一个接着一个地从地上捡起来石头，左右开弓，迅速地投了出去。那个生物退却了。米格尔抓起更多的石头向它的硬壳砸去。那只螃蟹慢了下来。

奏效了！

左，右。左，右。他想象着自己在电视前面，狠打着游戏里的那些外星螃蟹，但是，这次是真的！米格尔使出最后一点力气，把一块篮球那么

---

toss *v.* 扔

flinch *v.* 退缩

blast *v.* 狠打；猛踢

sailing right into the crab's mouth. Its huge claws crossed in front. Its antennas swayed.

Miguel froze.

And then the crab turned and crawled away.

"Ya-hoo!" He wished Trevon could have seen this victory.

Miguel reached down and untied the shoe stuck between the rocks. His foot slipped out, and he headed for the time machine. The time machine had to be the key to getting home. Miguel remembered that the time traveler had ended up back in his *laboratory* when he went backward in time. Maybe Miguel would end up back at home if

大的石头正好扔进了螃蟹的嘴里，它胡乱地在前面挥动着巨大的钳子。摇晃着触角。

米格尔愣在了那里。

然后那只螃蟹转过身，爬走了。

"太棒了！"他真希望特莱文能看见刚才的胜利。

米格尔俯下身，解开了那只卡在岩石缝里的鞋带。他把脚拔了出来，朝时光机走去。只有时光机才能带他回到家。米格尔想起来，故事结束的时候，时光穿梭者拉动了回到从前的操纵杆，回到了他的实验室。如果米格尔试着回到从前而不是走向未来，也许他就会回到家里。

laboratory *n.* 实验室

he tried to go backward in time instead of forward.

He sat in the *saddle* seat, pulled the other lever, and closed his eyes. He twirled. He spun. He could feel the air being *sucked* out of his *lungs*. Then suddenly, he was in the loft!

Miguel left the shop and ran home. He found Teresa dusting the living room.

"Nice of you to show up," she said.

Miguel walked over to her, grabbed the rag, and began to clean the bookshelf.

"Who are you?" she asked. "Not my brother—he doesn't work."

他坐在座椅上，拉动了另外一个操纵杆，闭上了眼睛。他旋转着。越转越快。他能感到肺里的空气都被转出去了。然后，突然间他回到了阁楼！

米格尔离开店里，跑回家。他看到了正在打扫房间的特丽莎。

“你终于出现了，”她说。

米格尔向她走过去，从她手中抓过抹布，开始擦书架。

“你是谁？”她问。“你不是我哥哥——他从不干活。”

---

saddle *n.* 座椅；车座

suck *v.* 吸

lung *n.* 肺

"Great-Grandpa Gallardo helped me out." Miguel thought of his fast-forward trip to the future, and sadness filled his heart. "Time is short. You never know how bright or dark the future will be." He dusted the books. "And hard work keeps you strong and smart." He smiled at Teresa.

"You're off the hook this time," she smiled back. "But only if I get to ***zap*** alien crabs while you work!"

"曾祖父盖拉多教育了我。"米格尔想到他的未来闪电之旅，悲从心来。"生命太短暂了。你永远不知道未来是什么样。"他掸着书上的灰尘。"努力工作会让你强壮聪明。"他对特丽莎微笑着说。

"你这次学乖了，"她笑着说。"不过，我可要在你干活时，玩这个打外星螃蟹的游戏了！"

---

zap *v.* 除掉

5

Arrows

The first arrow

Poloma was *tossing* her new ball high into the air when she discovered the first arrow in the forest. On that *particular* summer morning she was aiming for the sun, throwing the ball higher and higher, so when it came down and bounced away she had only herself to blame. The ball careened off a tree trunk, *bounced* over a log, and came to rest at the base of a huge *boulder*.

箭头

第一个箭头

帕洛玛正把她的新球高高地抛向空中，这时候，她发现了森林中的第一个箭头。在那个特殊的夏日清晨，她向着太阳的方向，把球高高地抛到空中，所以，当球落下来跳到了别处的时候，她只好自己去捡球。球砸在了一个树干上，从那蹦过圆木，钻进了一个巨大的卵石下面。

toss *v.* 抛
bounce *v.* 弹起
particular *adj.* 特殊的
boulder *n.* 卵石

She was digging the ball out from the heavy undergrowth when she noticed the arrow *carved* into the bottom of the *massive* rock.

Poloma grabbed her ball and raced home. Her grandfather was resting on the porch swing. His eyes were closed, and for a moment, she wondered whether she should wake him with the news.

"You've discovered something," he said softly when she was settled beside him. "I can tell by the way you're *fidgeting*."

"I've found an arrow, Papa!" Poloma kicked her feet, and the swing moved back and forth, making a gentle, reassuring, *squeaking* sound.

从这个重重的卵石下面掏球的时候，她注意到了一个刻在巨石底下的箭头。

帕洛玛抓着球跑回家。她的祖父正在门廊里的秋千上休息，他闭着眼睛，她想了一会儿，不知道是否该叫醒他，把这个消息告诉他。

"你发现了什么吧，"当她坐在祖父身边时，他柔声地说。"看你不安的样子我就知道。"

"我发现了一个箭头，爷爷！"帕洛玛的脚蹬了一下地，秋千前后摇荡，发出轻轻的、慵懒的、吱吱呀呀的声音。

---

carve *v.* 雕刻　　massive *adj.* 巨大的

fidget *v.* 坐立不安　　squeak *v.* 吱吱叫

"And where is this arrow that excites you so much?"

Poloma told her grandfather about the bouncing ball, the boulder, and the arrow that was carved at the bottom of it.

"Do you think the arrow is a glyph like the ones in my code books?" Poloma asked. "Maybe it's a ***Mayan hieroglyphic***. The Mayans used tiny pictures instead of words and letters. Maybe they carved that arrow," Poloma guessed.

Papa pulled himself out of the swing and smiled down at his granddaughter. "That's a very good question," he said. "But I doubt

---

"那么这个令你这么兴奋的箭头在哪儿呢？"

帕洛玛向祖父讲述了弹起的球，卵石还有它底下刻着的箭头。

"你觉得那个箭头会跟我密码书里的那些符号一样，是密码符号吗？"帕洛玛问。"或者它是玛雅的象形文字。玛雅人用小图画来代替文字和语言。也许他们刻下了那个箭头，"帕洛玛猜测着。

爷爷从秋千上下来，低头微笑地看着他的孙女。"这个问题问得很好，"他说。"但是，我不认为是玛雅人在这附近刻下了箭头。他们住在

Mayan *adj.* 玛雅人的　　hieroglyphic *n.* 象形文字

that the Mayans were carving rocks around here. The Mayans lived farther south, in Mexico and Central America. However, your arrow might very well be part of a code of some kind, but we might have to do some research to find out."

Poloma's grandfather knew a lot about codes. In fact, he had won a medal for his code work during World War II. Papa and other Native American Code Talkers had helped the United States and its *allies* win the war by sending secret messages.

"Will you tell me again, Papa?" Poloma *pleaded*. Poloma loved to hear the story of the Code Talkers, even though she had heard it many, many times before. She especially liked to hear about

遥远的南方，生活在墨西哥和中美洲。不过，你的箭头有可能是某种密码的一个符号，但是我们需要做进一步的调查，才能确定。"

帕洛玛的祖父很了解密码。实际上，他在二战期间曾经因为密码工作赢得了一枚勋章。爷爷和其他的印第安密码通讯员曾经通过发送秘密电文，帮助美国和其盟友赢得了战争。

"你能再给我讲一遍吗，爷爷？"帕洛玛恳求道。她喜欢听密码通讯员的故事，即使她以前已经听过很多很多遍了。她尤其喜欢听跟爷爷一样的密西西比乔克托密码通讯员的故事。

allies *n.* 盟军　　plead *v.* 请求

Mississippi Choctaw Code Talkers like her grandfather.

"Come," her grandfather said, as he took her hand and pulled her from the swing. "I think we should visit this *mysterious* arrow. I'll tell you about the Code Talkers while we walk."

As they made their way toward the boulder, Papa told Poloma the story of how he and other Code Talkers sent messages that no one could *interpret*.

Questions

"We spoke into walkie-talkie radios," he explained. "There was a Code Talker on each end, and we would only use Choctaw words that no one else could understand. Someone would give me

---

"来，"祖父说着拉着她的手，把她从秋千上拉下来。"我想我们应该去看看那个神秘的箭头。路上我会给你讲密码通讯员的故事。"

去找卵石的路上，爷爷给帕洛玛讲了他和其他的密码通讯员如何发出了无人能够破译的电文的故事。

问题

"我们通过手提无线电对讲机讲话，"他解释着。"每个对讲机那头都有一个密码通讯员，我们只使用乔克托语，没人能听懂。有人会把电文递给我，我会用乔克托语说出来。无线电另一端的密码通讯员会收到我

---

mysterious *adj.* 神秘的；陌生的

interpret *v.* 破译

the message that I was to pass on, and I would speak the words in Choctaw. The Code Talker on the other end would receive my message and translate it into English for the soldiers. If the enemy was listening in on the radio, they wouldn't be able to understand what we were saying."

Poloma and her grandfather were at the boulder now. They knelt down, and Poloma pointed to the *roughly* carved arrow. Wind and rain had smoothed the arrow's edges so much that Poloma might not have seen it had she not been paying attention.

"What do you think it means?" she asked.

Papa ran his finger back and *forth* over the carving. "I'm not sure,"

的电文，把它翻译成英语，告诉其他的士兵。如果敌人正在通过无线电偷听，他们也不会听懂我们说的是什么。"

帕洛玛和祖父现在已经来到了那块卵石前。他们跪在地上，帕洛玛指着那个粗糙地刻在上面的箭头。风雨已经磨光了箭头的边缘，以至于帕洛玛如果不留意的话，也许就发现不了它。

"你觉得它是什么意思？"她问。

爷爷用手指来回抚摸着这个箭头。"我不太确定。"他说。"这个刻

---

roughly *adv.* 粗糙地

forth *adv.* 向前；向某处

he said. "It's a very old carving, but it's hard to determine its age. It takes a lot of work to finger out how old a carving is."

"How could people know?" Poloma asked.

"Well, there are many ways. Remember the cave paintings we saw last summer, and the old *fossils* and bones we saw at the Natural History Museum? Scientists use a method called carbon dating to finger out how old those things are."

"Can we use it to tell how old our arrow is?" Poloma asked.

"Maybe someone could date the plants in the *cracks* nearest to the carving," Papa told her. "But let's try something else. Let's try studying the arrow as it is."

痕应经很久了，很难确定它的年代。人们需要做很多工作才能确定它是什么时候刻上去的。"

"人们是怎么知道的呢？"帕洛玛问。

"你看，有很多方法。记得我们去年夏天看到的那个山洞里的壁画，还有在国家历史博物馆我们看到的那些化石和骨头吗？科学家们利用一种叫碳测法的方法去推断这些东西的年代。"

"我们能用这种方法测出这个箭头的年代吗？"帕洛玛问。

"也许有人能根据箭头附近裂缝里的植物的年代推算出来，"爷爷告诉她。"不过，我们还是来看点其他的东西吧。我们来研究一下这个箭

---

fossil *n.* 化石　　crack *n.* 裂缝

Poloma stared at the arrow for a long time. Suddenly, she had an idea.

"I know!" she shouted. "How about if we consider where the arrow is pointing?"

The arrow was pointing toward another boulder nearby. Poloma and Papa followed it, and found the second arrow almost *immediately*. The second arrow was pointing in the same direction as the first, and so they followed that one too. It led to another boulder, and another arrow, which led to yet another, and then another arrow.

头本身。"

帕洛玛盯着箭头看了很久。突然，她有了一个想法。

"我知道了！"她大声叫道。"我们看一下箭头指示的方向怎么样？"

这个箭头指着的是附近另外一块卵石。帕洛玛和爷爷沿着箭头的方向，几乎马上就找到了第二个箭头。它跟第一个箭头指的是同一个方向。于是，他们便接着往下找。箭头把他们带到了另外一块卵石前，在那里他们又发现了一个，然后又发现了一个，接着又是一个。

---

immediately *adv.* 马上

There were six arrows in all.

"What do you think it means, Papa?" Poloma asked as she ran her fingers over the sixth arrow.

"I think it means we should look for the next arrow," Papa laughed. "The arrows are sending us somewhere, and I can't wait to see where."

They continued on in the direction the arrows had been leading them, but saw no more boulders. The meaning of the arrows had been ***confusing***, but what came next was even more ***perplexing***. The arrows led them straight toward a stream.

"What should we do?" Poloma asked.

一共有六个箭头。

"你觉得它是什么意思，爷爷？"帕洛玛摩挲着第六个箭头问。

"我想它指示我们去寻找下一个箭头，"爷爷笑着说。"这些箭头在领着我们去一个地方，我都等不及去看看了。"

他们继续朝箭头所指的方向前进，但并没有看到什么卵石。这些箭头已经很令人迷惑了，可接下来的事更令人费解。这些箭头把他们径直领到了一条小溪前。

"我们怎么办？"帕洛玛问。

---

confuse *v.* 把……弄迷糊；使困惑

perplexing *adj.* 令人困惑的

"I guess we should cross the stream. It looks very *shallow*, so if we *tiptoe* from stone to stone perhaps we'll find another arrow on the other side. Hold my hand tight; we'll cross together." Papa said.

Answers

They crossed the stream, holding hands, stepping carefully. When they reached the other side they almost crashed into the next boulder. It was hidden in a *grove* of old *pine* trees.

"Do you think there's anything carved on it?" Poloma asked.

"Let's take a look," Papa said.

They knelt down together, side by side, and examined the boulder. At first they couldn't find an arrow or any other carving, and

---

"我猜我们得穿过这条小溪。它看起来很浅，所以我们踮起脚，踩着石头穿过去，也许我们会在小溪那边找到其他的箭头。抓紧我的手，我们一起过去。"爷爷说。

答案

他们牵着手，小心翼翼地穿过小溪。他们来到了溪水的另一边，差点撞到一个卵石上。它隐藏在一片古老的松树林里。

"你觉得这块卵石上面会刻着东西吗？"帕洛玛问。

"我们看看吧，"爷爷说。

---

shallow *adj.* 浅的
grove *n.* 树林
tiptoe *v.* 踮着脚走
pine *n.* 松树

they were about to give up when Poloma *screeched*.

"I found something! I found something!" she shouted, as she leaned closer to the boulder and *scraped* off some *moss* with her fingers. "Look, Papa! It's not an arrow at all—a whole bunch of letters are carved into the bottom of the boulder! I wonder if we can make them out."

"I'm afraid you'll have to read them to me," Papa stood up slowly and *rubbed* his knees. "My eyes are too old to make out tiny letters that have been hidden behind overgrown underbrush for such a long time. I'm afraid my knees aren't too good either."

他们一起并排跪下，仔细地审视着。一开始他们并没发现任何箭头或雕刻，就在他们打算放弃的时候，帕洛玛叫了起来。

“我看到了点儿东西！我看到了点儿东西！”她一边喊一边贴近卵石，用手指刮掉了一些苔藓。“看，爷爷！根本不是箭头，岩石底下刻着的是一整串字母！我不知道我们能否看得懂。”

“恐怕你得把它们读给我听，”爷爷慢慢地站起身，揉了揉膝盖。“我的眼睛看不清那些细小的字母，它们藏在岩石的底下太久了。我的膝盖也不是很舒服。”

---

screech *v.* 尖叫
moss *n.* 苔藓
scrape *v.* 刮
rub *v.* 揉

Poloma leaned closer to the boulder and studied the letters. It took her a long time, but she was finally able to read them all.

"They don't make any sense," she said. "I'll say them to you, but I don't think they mean anything at all."

Poloma read each letter out loud, very slowly.

"g p m m p x u i f e s j o l j o h h p v s e"

When she was finished she said, "Maybe they're a code. Do you think they could be a *code*, Papa?"

"Read them again," Papa said. "Maybe I can make some sense

帕洛玛贴近卵石，仔细地辨认着那些字母。她看了很久，不过最后她还是把它们都认了出来。

“它们没什么意义，”她说。“我把它们读给你听，不过我想它们根本说不通。”

帕洛玛大声地慢慢地把每个字母都大声地读了出来：

“g p m m p x u i f e s j o l j o h h p v s e”

读完后她说，“也许，它们是密码。你觉得它们会是密码吗，爷爷？”

“再读一遍，”爷爷说。“如果你再读一遍，也许我能分析出点什

---

code *n.* 密码

of them if you read them again."

Poloma said the letters again, and then she repeated them one more time. As she read, she could hear her grandfather's footsteps. He was pacing slowly through the dead leaves and pine ***needles***. Papa always paced when he had something important to mull over.

"Do they mean anything to you?" she asked when she was done.

"Indeed they do," her grandfather said, still pacing. "Indeed they do."

"What do you think the letters mean?"

"I'm not exactly sure," Papa told her." But I think it's a ***cipher***, and

---

么。”

帕洛玛又把字母说了一遍，接着又重复了一次。读这些字母的时候，她能听到祖父的脚步声。他在落叶和松针上慢慢地踱着步。爷爷在思索的时候，总是这样踱步。

“你看出点什么了吗？”读完后她问。

“它们一定意味着什么，”祖父说，仍然踱着步。“它们一定意味着什么。”

“你觉得这些字母是什么意思？”

“我不是很确定，”爷爷对她说，“但我想这是一句密语，我想我能

---

needle *n.* 针

cipher *n.* 密码

I think I recognize it."

Poloma knew what a cipher was. It was a code that *substituted* letters or numbers for the real letters in a message.

"Ciphers like that one have been used in many wars to keep the enemy from learning about battle plans," Papa explained.

Cracking the Code

"Did you use a cipher in the war?" Poloma asked.

"I saw them used in World War II. The Germans had a very clever machine called the Enigma machine that substituted letters for other letters. But the first substitution cipher was invented by Julius

破译它。"

帕洛玛知道密语是什么。是用一些别的字母或数字代替信息中真正的字母。

"像是那些人们在许多战争中使用的，避免被敌人了解作战计划的那种密语，"爷爷解释道。

破解密码

"你们在战争中使用过密码吗？"帕洛玛问。

"我看到过人们在二战中使用过。德国人有一种非常智能的机器，叫密码机，它能用代码取代字母。不过，第一套密码是由尤里乌斯·凯撒在

substitute *v.* 代替

Caesar more than 2,000 years ago."

"I wonder if these letters were used in a war too," Poloma said.

Papa had to think about that. He paced for a very long time and then he stopped beside his granddaughter and cleared his *throat*.

"I think I remember something," he said. "As you know, a great war took place right around here."

"The Civil War, right, Papa?" Poloma asked. "When did the war take place?"

"About 150 years ago, the Civil War was fought to free the slaves in the South. I think I recall reading that the soldiers and *spies* in the

---

两千多年前发明的。"

"我想知道这些字母是否也是战争中使用过，"帕洛玛说。

爷爷还得再仔细想想。他踱了好久的步，然后在他的孙女旁边停了下来，清了清喉咙说。

"我想起了一些事，"他说。"你知道，就在这附近曾经爆发过一场伟大的战争。"

"内战，对吗，爷爷？"帕洛玛问，"这场战争是什么时候发生的呢？"

---

throat *n.* 喉咙

spy *n.* 间谍

North used a special cipher."

"Do you remember what it was, Papa?"

"It was sort of like the Caesar Cipher like the Caesar Cipher. Read me the letters again."

Poloma read the letters slowly.

"g p m m p x u i f e s j o l j o h h p v s e"

Papa shook his head and placed a ***gentle*** hand on his granddaughter's shoulder.

"You forgot the spaces," he said, "Read the letters again, and don't forget the spaces between the words."

"大约150年前，内战是为了解放南方的奴隶。我想起来读到过北方的士兵和间谍曾经使用过一种特殊的密码。"

"你记得是什么密码吗，爷爷？"

"一种类似凯撒密码的密码。再给我读一遍那些字母。"

帕洛玛慢慢地读出了那些字母：

"g p m m p x u i f e s j o l j o h h p v s e"

爷爷摇了摇头，把手温和地放在孙女的肩上。

"你忘记了空格，"他说，"重新读一遍，别忘了单词之间的空格。"

---

gentle *adj.* 温和的

Poloma read the letters. This time she was careful to pause whenever she saw a space.

"g p m m p x u i f e s j o l j o h h p v s e"

She was just about to ask her grandfather what the letters meant, when she noticed something in the cipher that she had seen in codes she had ***deciphered*** before. Most sentences contain at least one small common word, and this one was no different.

"I think I see some interesting letters," she said. "Let's say the letters form words. One of the words has three letters. Let's guess that it's a common word ..."

"... like and?"

帕洛玛又读了一遍。这次她很小心地在空格的地方停顿了一下：

"g p m m p x u i f e s j o l j o h h p v s e"

她正打算问祖父这些字母的意思，这时，她在这句密语中发现了一种现象，这种现象也存在于她曾经破解过的密语中。大多数句子都至少会出现一个短的常见的词汇，这句密语也不例外。

"我想我看见了一些有趣的字母，"她说。"让我们看看构成单词的字母。其中的一个词有三个字母。我们假定它是一个常用词汇……"

"……比如and？"

---

decipher *v.* 破译

"Or the," Poloma suggested. "There has to be one common word in a sentence."

Poloma and Papa were quiet for several minutes, as they thought about the three letters.

"I don't think it's and," Papa said. "The letters don't make sense."

"But it could be the," Poloma said. "Maybe the letters uif stands for the in some way."

Papa was smiling now. "You are a very smart girl," he said. "What letter comes before u in the ***alphabet***?"

"T," Poloma said. "And the letter h comes before i, and the letter e comes before f. This is a substitute letter cipher, Papa!"

"或者the，"帕洛玛说。"句子中一定有个常用词汇。"

帕洛玛和爷爷静静地想了几分钟，他们在想那个三个字母组成的词。

"我觉得不是and，"爷爷说。"这些字母说不通。"

"不过有可能是the，"帕洛玛说。"也许u i f按照某种规律代表的是the。"

爷爷现在笑了。"你真是个聪明的女孩，"他说。"字母表中u前面是什么字母？"

"T，"帕洛玛说。"i前面的是h，f在e的前面。这是一套替代密码，爷爷！"

---

alphabet *n.* 字母表

"Yes! I remember now! During the Civil War some northern spies and soldiers used a code called the advance cipher. They advanced each letter one letter of the alphabet."

The Drinking Gourd

Once they had cracked the code, it was easy to read the message.

"Do you know what it says?" Poloma asked.

"I do know what it says. Do you know what it says?"

"I know what it says, Papa. It says 'Follow the Drinking Gourd.' But, I don't know what's meaning, do you know?"

Papa *chuckled* and sat down on a *hollow* log. "We've made quite a discovery," he said. "We have found six arrows pointing in the same

---

"对！我现在记起来了！在内战期间，一些北方的间谍和士兵使用过一种提前密码。他们把字母表中的每个字母都提前了。"

北斗七星

一旦他们破译了密码，就很容易读出了这条信息。

"你知道这句话说的是什么吗？"帕洛玛问。

"我知道，你知道吗？"

"我知道，爷爷。它说的是'沿着北斗七星的方向'。但是，我不明白是什么意思，你知道吗？"

爷爷笑着坐在了一个中空的圆木上。"我们已经找到了很多线索，"

---

chuckle *v.* 轻声笑　　　　hollow *adj.* 空心的

direction. If someone followed the arrows they would reach this boulder, and they would reach this cipher. I wonder if the arrows and the cipher were carved during the Civil War."

Papa was pacing again now, and Poloma could tell that he was mulling things over in his mind.

"Before the end of the war," he said, "many slaves wanted to escape to *freedom* in the north. They followed what was called the Underground Railroad. It wasn't really a *railroad*. It was just a series of routes and directions and safe houses that led the slaves northward. Some slaves who had escaped returned to help other slaves."

他说。“我们已经找到了指向同一方向的六个箭头。如果有人沿着箭头指示的方向走，就会找到卵石，他们就会看到密语。我想知道这些箭头和密语是不是内战期间刻上去的。”

爷爷又在踱步了，帕洛玛知道他正在思索。

“在战争结束前，”他说，“许多奴隶都想逃往北方，寻求自由。他们沿着一条被称为地下铁路的路线走。那不是一条真的铁路，只是一系列的路线和方向，还有一些能把奴隶带到北方的安全地点。一些逃到北方的奴隶也返回南方帮助其他的奴隶。”

---

freedom *n.* 自由

railroad *n.* 铁路

"But who carved the arrows, Papa?"

"I'm not sure if we'll ever know that," Papa said. "It might have been a northern spy trying to help. It might have been a returning slave who had learned the cipher in the north. Or maybe it had nothing to do with the war. Who knows? Maybe some children were playing a game."

"Did slaves ever carve directions in trees or rocks?" Poloma asked.

"I've never heard of it happening, but every day people find new information about the Underground Railroad. Just *recently* someone

---

"可是谁刻了那些箭头呢，爷爷？"

"我不是很确定我们能否找到答案，"爷爷说。"有可能是想要帮忙的北方间谍。有可能是在北方学会了密码，又返回南方的奴隶。又或者它跟战争无关。谁知道呢？也许是一些孩子的游戏。"

"奴隶们曾经在树上或岩石上刻方向吗？"帕洛玛问。

"我从来没听说过，但是每天人们都会发现关于地下铁路的新信息。就在最近有人在爱荷华州的一所房子里发现了密道和密室。奴隶在去北方

---

recently *adv.* 最近

discovered a hidden *tunnel* and a secret room in a house in Iowa where slaves hid out on the way north."

"What does 'Follow the Drinking Gourd' mean?" Poloma asked.

"The Drinking Gourd is the group of seven stars now called the Big Dipper, which can always be found in the northern sky of the United States. Slaves followed the Drinking Gourd from safe house to safe house, until, finally, they reached freedom."

The sun was beginning to set, and tiny slivers of light were *flickering* through the branches. Poloma took her flashlight from her backpack, turned it on, and took her grandfather's hand.

的路上，曾经在那里藏身。"

"'沿着北斗七星的方向'是什么意思？"帕洛玛问。

"北斗七星是一个由七颗星星组成的星座，现在叫北斗星座。它总是出现在美国北面的天空中。奴隶们沿着北斗七星的方向走，从一个安全地走到另外一个安全地点，直到最终获得自由。"

太阳开始落山了，树林中只能看见一点点微弱的光。帕洛玛从背包里拿出手电，打开，拉着祖父的手。

---

tunnel *n.* 地道　　flicker *v.* 闪烁

By the time they were on the other side of the stream, the sun had *disappeared*. Poloma stopped and studied the sky.

"Are you looking for the Drinking Gourd?" her grandfather asked.

"There it is!" Poloma was pointing to the bright shape in the sky. "Shall we follow it?"

"It's your decision. Are we heading north?"

Poloma had to think about that for a minute. The Drinking Gourd would lead them back across the stream, past the boulder with the cipher, and on and on to places north.

他们到达小溪另一边的时候，太阳完全看不见了。帕洛玛停下来，望着天空。

“你在找北斗七星吗？”祖父问。

“在那里！”帕洛玛指着天空中一个星座说。“我们沿着它的方向走吗？”

“你决定吧。我们去北方吗？”

帕洛玛想了一会儿。北斗七星将会把他们领回到小溪的另一边，经过刻着密语的卵石，一直领到北方。

---

disappear *v.* 消失

"We need to go south, Papa."

Poloma and Papa turned. They moved slowly, like *creeping* night creatures. The light from Poloma's flashlight led them away from the North Star, past the arrows pointing the other way, out of the woods, and home.

"我们得往南走，爷爷。"

帕洛玛和爷爷转身往南走。他们像夜晚的爬行动物一样，走得很慢。帕洛玛手电的光亮带着他们远离了北极星，走过了指向相反方向的箭头，走出树林，走回了家。

---

creep *v.* 爬行

6

Westward Journey

1848, west of Independence, Missouri

"How in all creation did I land here?" thought eleven-year-old Jessie Townsend. The wheels of his family's covered *wagon* rolled over the *uneven* ruts that marked the beginning of a 2,000-mile wagon-train journey west. Oregon Country promised flowers that bloomed all year, free land ripe for farming, and rivers and streams overflowing with fish; but, none of this bounty mattered to Jessie.

西进之旅

1848年，密苏里州的西部独立运动

"怎么来到这个地方？"杰西·汤森这个11岁的小男孩想不明白。他们全家坐着有篷的牛车，走在崎岖不平的路上，踏上了长达2000英里的西进之旅。据说俄勒冈花开四季，遍地沃土，水中鱼满为患；这些杰西

wagon *n.* 小手推车　　uneven *adj.* 不平坦的

His closest friends and favorite fishing hole remained in Ohio.

With a clenched jaw and downward-fixed eyes, Jessie *jostled* around — back and forth, up and down — on one of the 36 wagons slowly rolling west, and refused to see the beauty of the wide-open spaces. "Why did we ever leave Ohio?" he thought as he leaped down from the wagon. With slumping shoulders, he then grabbed a pebble from his shoe and forcefully flung it to the ground.

Huddled together inside the oxen-pulled wagon were Jessie's mother and eight-year-old sister. His mother and sister looked alike with their brightly-colored cotton dresses and *bonnets* that his mother had hand-sewn. Jessie and his father looked like mirror images in the grey cotton pants, grey shirts, and hats that Jessie's mother had

---

都不关心，因为他最要好的朋友和最得意的钓鱼洞都留在了俄亥俄。

杰西撅着嘴，眉头紧锁，在车里前后左右上下颠簸。这个由36辆牛车组成的车队，缓缓地西进。杰西没有心情欣赏车外旷野美景。他跳下马车，心里想道，“我们到底为什么要离开俄亥俄呢？”他很是无精打采，从鞋里抠出一个石子，狠狠地摔在地上。

杰西与妈妈还有一个8岁的妹妹一起挤在这辆牛车里。妈妈和妹妹打扮一样，都穿着妈妈手缝的亮色的棉布衣裙和帽子。他和爸爸穿着一样，可以互相当镜子了——都穿着灰布长裤、灰色衬衫和帽子，也都是妈妈做

---

jostle *v.* 推挤　　bonnet *n.* 童帽

also sewn. Jessie and his father routinely walked side by side during the 10 to 15 miles the wagon train travelled each day.

In the wagon following, another eleven-year-old-a blond-haired, blue-eyed girl named Bessie noticed Jessie walking on the flat *prairie* beside his family's wagon. She thought he looked about her age and wondered whether he might be interested in playing with her and Wag.

Bessie jumped down from the wagon and threw Wag's favorite ball into the high prairie grass in the general direction of the boy. "Come on, Wag," Bessie coaxed, "go fetch."

Wag, a four-year-old golden *retriever*, took off in an instant. He

---

的。每天杰西和爸爸都要肩并肩在车旁走上10到15英里。

后面的车里有个金发蓝眼名叫贝茜的11岁小女孩，看到这个与她年龄相仿的男孩在车旁的草地上走，想知道他愿意不愿意与她和微格一起玩儿。

贝茜跳下牛车，把微格最喜欢的球向男孩那边的高草地抛去。“微格，去，拿回来！”她怂恿道。

微格是一条4岁大的金色寻回犬，听到命令箭一般地冲出去。他跳起

---

prairie *n.* 草原

retriever *n.* 寻回犬

cavorted like a puppy as he sprang forward, hurtled toward the ball, retrieved it, and presented it back to Bessie before she could take more than one step. The boy ahead barely noticed the ruckus created by the energetic dog's mad dash for his toy. Bessie's attempt to *snare* the boy's attention failed.

"Maybe he doesn't care beans for dogs," Bessie thought. Then, Wag distracted her by nudging her hand and dropping the ball into it. Though Wag was a dog, he moved as quickly as a rabbit and could play for hours and hours and never tire. Bessie likened herself more to a *tortoise* than a hare and was always first to end their fetching games.

来像条小狗，一下子扑过去，贝茜一步还没有迈出去，他已经把球给她叼回来了。但是她想引起杰西注意的努力却失败了。男孩几乎没有注意到这边由这条生龙活虎的狗引起的骚动。

“也许他压根就不喜欢狗，”贝茜猜测。微格蹭蹭她的手，把球交给她，她才回过神来。虽然它是狗，跑起来却像兔子一样快，玩上几个小时也不累。比起兔子，贝茜宁愿把自己比成乌龟，总是她首先在这样取猎物的游戏中败下阵来。

snare *v.* 捕捉

tortoise *n.* 乌龟

As Bessie walked beside the wagon a few days later, she began to feel dizzy, and the feeling worsened as the day grew longer. "Uh-oh, my stomach is doing flip-flops," she thought. "And my head is beginning to feel like flour ***kneaded*** into pie dough." Bessie didn't want to be treated like a baby and be ***confined*** to the wagon—so she hid her illness as long as possible.

At dinnertime, however, when the wagon train set up camp for the night. Bessie could no longer fake feeling well. When her mother, Sarah, caught a ***glimpse*** of her in the firelight, she immediately felt Bessie's forehead and realized that her daughter was burning up with fever.

几天后，贝茜在车外走时觉得头晕目眩，走的时间越长，她就越是晕得厉害。“胃在翻山蹈海，头像揉成的馅饼面团。”她自己想。但贝茜不想待在车里被当成孩子一样照顾，所以她尽可能地不让别人发现她的不适。

然而，当车队开始宿营，吃晚饭的时候。她再也装不下去了。妈妈莎拉借着火光瞟了她一眼，摸了一下她的额头，马上意识到女儿发烧了。

knead *v.* 揉；捏

confine *v.* 限制

glimpse *n.* 一瞥；一看

"Go lie down, Bessie," Sarah ordered. "I'll bring you a cupful of bitters to drink. I want you lying on that *mattress* until you're feeling better."

"Yes, ma'am, but what about my *responsibilities* to Wag? Who will take care of him?"

"I'll feed him and give him water," Sarah said.

"Yes, but who will entertain him? He's used to me playing with him every day."

"I'm sorry, Bessie, but none of us has the time to watch him or play with him," said her father, William. "Don't worry. He'll be fine."

"快躺下，贝茜，"她命令道。"我给你拿杯药喝。躺在垫子上，感觉好些再起来。"

"好的，妈妈，但是微格怎么办？谁照顾他？"

"我喂它吃喝，"莎拉说。

"但是谁陪它玩呢，它每天习惯和我玩了。"

"贝茜，很抱歉，我们谁也没有时间照看它，陪它玩，"爸爸威廉说。"不过不用担心，它不会有事的。"

---

mattress *n.* 垫子

responsibility *n.* 责任

That night, Bessie slept *fitfully* as her fever climbed ever higher. *Plaguing* her sleep were *nightmares* of Wag being lonely, wandering the vast prairie, and searching for her from far behind the wagon train.

Two mornings later as the wagon train prepared to break camp, Jessie walked up to Bessie's father.

"Uh, pardon me, sir, where is the little girl who plays with the dog? Is she in good health?"

"I'm afraid our daughter is ill with fever, so she's abed inside the wagon."

晚上，贝茜烧得更厉害。因此睡得很不安稳，老是梦到微格独自在草原上游荡，跟在车队后面到处找她。

两天后的一个早晨，当车队停下来休息的时候，杰西向贝茜的父亲走过来。

"打扰您，先生，请问和小狗玩的那个小女孩在哪儿？她身体好吗？"

"我女儿发烧了，在车里卧床休息。"

---

fitfully *adv.* 断断续续地
plague *v.* 烦恼
nightmare *n.* 噩梦

"Oh, sorry," said Jessie *apologetically*, knowing others in the wagon train were suffering from a similar *affliction*. "Where's her dog?" he asked.

"He sleeps next to her most of the day," answered Bessie's father.

"I mean no *disrespect*, but is he getting any exercise?" Jessie asked. "Is anyone paying attention to him when he's *rambling* around?"

"We're too busy to worry about that, I'm afraid," said Sarah as she reloaded the breakfast supplies.

"很抱歉，"杰西满是歉意地说。他知道在整个车队里还有其他人也在遭受类似病情的折磨。"她的狗呢？"他问道。

"它大部分时间都躺在贝茜身边睡觉，"她父亲答道。

"素我冒昧，它有得到训练吗？它溜达的时候有人照看吗？"男孩问。

"我们太忙了，恐怕没人能顾及这些，"莎拉边说边把早餐的东西装上车。

---

apologetically *adv.* 歉意地

affliction *n.* 痛苦

disrespect *n.* 不尊重

ramble *v.* 漫步

"Well, maybe I could come by and tend to his exercise each day," offered Jessie, "at least until your daughter is feeling better."

"Well, that would be very kind of you," said Sarah. "Bessie would truly *appreciate* your taking an interest in Wag."

"Oh, it's no trouble, ma'am," said Jessie. "I'll come back later this afternoon to tend to him."

That night, Bessie's illness became as severe as her parents had ever seen. Chills shook Bessie's body as Sarah spoon – fed her all the medicine they had to make her well. It seemed as though nothing improved her *condition*. Earlier that morning, an elderly woman had died from sickness.

"也许我可以过来每天训练它，"杰西主动提出，"至少直到您女儿好起来。"

"那太好了，"莎拉说，"贝茜会非常感激你照看微格的。"

"一点都不麻烦，"杰西说，"下午晚些时候我过来照顾它。"

晚上，贝茜的病情恶化，是她的父母见过的最严重的一次。她全身打战，为了让她好起来，妈妈把能治她病的药都拿了出来，一勺一勺喂她。但似乎不起什么作用。就在那天早上，一位老太太病逝了。

---

appreciate *v.* 感激　　condition *n.* 状况

Sarah could not bear the thought of losing her child. Bessie awoke *delirious* several times in the night but didn't notice her mother's tear-stained cheeks. About an hour before dawn, Bessie's fever broke. Sarah's shoulders shook as she wept with joy, and William comforted her.

After a brief amount of *restful* sleep, Sarah and William had their team of oxen *plodding* along the trail when a thunderous boom echoed across the countryside.

"Hurry, circle the wagons," shouted the trail leader from a few wagons ahead. Bessie's parents hurried to do as they were told though their daughter was *oblivious* to the trouble heading in their

---

要失去女儿，莎拉不忍心冒出这种想法。晚上，贝茜从昏迷中醒来几次，并没有注意到妈妈满脸泪痕。天亮前的一个小时，贝茜的烧退了。莎拉喜极而泣，威廉过来安慰她。

莎拉和威廉终于可以安心地睡一会儿了，但很快他们又上路了，车队缓缓前行，这时从远方传来轰隆隆的声音，回荡在旷野中。

“赶快，把车围成一个圈，”前边的车队长喊道。贝茜的父母赶忙照做，而此时他们的女儿并不知道麻烦马上要来了。“快，围成圈。有不速

---

delirious *adj.* 昏迷的

restful *adj.* 安心的

plod *v.* 缓慢地走

oblivious *adj.* 不注意的

direction. “Circle the wagons. Unwelcome company’s about to charge past us. Round up the animals and the children. Make sure everyone and everything is accounted for. We don’t have much time!”

Although he advised everyone not to *panic*, it was clear in listening to the voice of the wagon-train leader, that he too was frightened. His warning traveled like wildfire throughout the train, and everyone scurried to direct their wagons into a circular pattern, placing the oxen in the center so the vital animals wouldn’t *stampede*.

Just as the circle had barely been completed, a huge herd of

之客要向我们奔来。把牲口和孩子都围起来。照顾好每一个人，每一样东西。没有多少时间了！”

虽然他告诉大家不要慌，但是可以听出来他也害怕。他的警告像野火一样从队前传到队尾，大家赶忙把车围成圈，牛放在中间，以免这些对他们来说最重要的牲口遭到践踏。

这个圈几乎刚刚完成，一大群棕色毛皮的庞然大物呼啸而来。保护圈内的每个人都感到大地在颤抖，铺天盖地的水牛踢起层层尘土，笼罩了一

panic *v.* 惊慌

stampede *v.* 惊窜

enormous creatures with brown, *shaggy* coats rushed around it. Everyone inside the protection of the ring felt the earth shake as countless buffalo kicked up a blanket of dust that enveloped everything for hours.

Everyone literally held their breath as much as possible, and no one dared move outside the circle until the wagon-train leader signaled that every single buffalo in the herd had passed by.

When it was again quiet enough to hear the call of a bird, the pioneers felt it was safe to *venture* out. They moved their wagons back to their usual single-file line and began heading west once again. "Where's Wag?" asked a weak voice from inside the wagon.

切，几个小时才散去。

每个人都尽可能地屏住呼吸，没有人敢走出圈外，直到队长示意水牛群全部走过去了。

一切又恢复平静，又可以听到鸟的叫声，一些胆大的人感到安全了，便壮着胆子走出来。和往常一样，他们把车队排成一列，又踏上西进之旅。“我的微格呢？”一个微弱的声音从车内传出。

---

enormous *adj.* 极大的
shaggy *adj.* 蓬乱的
venture *v.* 冒险

"I don't know," said William. "I haven't seen him since before the buffalo ***stampede***."

"Oh no, you don't suppose he got scared and ran off... do you?" asked Bessie.

"I don't know, Bessie, but I'm afraid that's very possible," answered her father.

"Well, I'm going to go search for him," she said with ***purpose***.

"No, you're not. Your fever may have broken overnight, but you're far from well. I don't want you wandering about, getting dizzy again, and falling and hurting yourself or worse."

"不知道，"威廉说，"水牛群来之前就没看见它。"

"不要，您不是说它受到惊吓，跑丢了吧？"贝茜追问。

"我也不清楚，贝茜，不过这很可能，"爸爸回答。

"那我要去找它，"贝茜坚决地说。

"你不要去。昨晚你烧是退了，但是还没有完全好。我不想让你到处走，又该晕倒了，病情会加重。"

---

stampede *n.* 惊跑；狂奔

purpose *n.* 决心

"I don't care about any of that. I only care about Wag. Please, you know I have to find him. We can't leave him out here alone." Visions of Bessie's nightmare haunted her.

"We don't really have a choice," said her father sadly, wishing he'd done more to discourage his daughter from becoming so *attached* to an animal.

"I think I have what you're looking for," said Jessie, who seemed to appear out of thin air with Wag trailing along behind him.

"Wag, boy, you're safe!" *exclaimed* Bessie as color returned to her cheeks for an instant, and she climbed down from the wagon

---

"我才不管这些。我就关心我的微格。求求你，我必须找到它。不能把它独自留在这里。"噩梦的情景又浮现在她眼前。

"我们别无选择，"爸爸难过地说，一心希望自己能使女儿不要对动物如此痴迷。

"我想我找到了你要找的东西，"杰西说，他不知从哪里冒了出来，微格就跟在他后面。

"微格，宝贝，你没事了！"贝茜惊喜地叫道，双颊立刻恢复血色，

---

attached *adj.* 依恋的　　exclaim *v.* 惊叫

despite her mother's protests.

Jessie explained that he'd found Wag hiding under his family's wagon just before the buffalo herd stormed past. Wag nearly bolted out into the *herd*, but Jessie was able to *coax* him into the wagon, where he was content to play tug-of-war with a section of old rope Jessie had.

Bessie scratched Wag behind his ears and looked *warily* at Jessie, who couldn't help but crack a giant *grin* as Wag started to lick every inch of Bessie's face.

Bessie couldn't help but giggle, which set Jessie to hooting. Wag happily swished his tail back and forth, and nearly knocked Bessie

---

她不顾妈妈反对，爬下车来。

杰西解释说就在水牛群冲来之前，他发现微格躲在一家人的车下面。要不是杰西把它哄进车里，它就差点冲进水牛群里了，在车里它安心地与杰西的一段绳子玩起了拔河游戏。

贝茜轻挠着微格的耳背，小心地打量着杰西，杰西看着微格舔遍贝茜整张脸，忍不住咧嘴笑了。

贝茜也忍不住咯咯笑起来，这让杰西呵呵笑出声来。微格高兴地摇着尾巴，它热情的舌浴快把贝茜推倒了。

---

herd *n.* 牛群

coax *v.* 哄骗

warily *adv.* 小心地

grin *n.* 咧嘴一笑

over with his *enthusiastic* tongue bath.

"I don't know what I would have done if you hadn't saved Wag," said Bessie, serious once more.

"I know exactly how you feel," Jessie said, pausing to remember the friends he'd most likely never see again.

"When you're feeling better, how about the three of us play fetch together?" he asked *tentatively*.

"You bet," agreed Bessie, figuring that if Wag thought this boy was all right, she could give him a chance, too. Having another friend with whom to spend time might make the demanding journey ahead a little easier to take — for both of them.

"如果不是你救了微格，我真不知道我会干出什么事，"贝茜又认真起来。

"我特别了解你的感受，"杰西说，他不禁又想起了他那些好朋友们，很可能再也见不到了。

"等你好起来，我们三个一起玩取猎物游戏，好不好？"杰西试探着问。

"一定，"贝茜答道。如果微格认为这个男孩不错，她想可以给他一次机会。多一个朋友一起走过这个艰难的旅程，也许会更好过些——对两个人都是。

---

enthusiastic *adj.* 热情的 tentatively *adv.* 试探地

7

The Lost Dutchman

CHAPTER 1: The Legend

The class began just like any other. Mr. Martinez collected homework from his fourth grade students. He asked them questions about their assigned readings. Then he talked about the next topic in Arizona history: the gold rush of the 1800s. ***Prospectors*** came to the desert hoping to find gold and silver in the mountains.

迷失的荷兰人

第一章：传说

这一天，像平常一样上课。马丁内斯老师收来了四年级学生们的作业。又让他们根据规定的阅读内容回答问题。接着他讲到了亚利桑那州历史上的另一个话题：19世纪的淘金热。探矿者们来到沙漠，希望在山上找到黄金或白银。

prospector *n.* 探矿者

legend *n.* 传说

"One *legend* in particular has captured the imaginations of Arizonans, even to this day," Mr. Martinez said. "This is the story of the Lost Dutchman's Gold Mine. You see, in 1868, a farmer moved to Phoenix. He had dreams of striking it rich. One day, he decided to trade in his farming tools for *picks* and *shovels*. He and his burro used to disappear for days at a time into the Superstition Mountains. These mountains are still just outside of our city."

Mr. Martinez pointed to the map on the wall. "Here in these *canyons*, this man was rumored to have found gold. Every so often, he emerged from the mountains with big *chunks* of solid gold. People tried to follow him, but he always gave them the slip. His name was Jacob Waltz."

"特别引起亚利桑那州人向往的是其中的一个传说，即使到今天也是一样，" 马丁内斯老师说。"这就是关于'迷失的荷兰人金矿'的故事。你们知道吗？在1868年，一位农民来到菲尼克斯。他一心想发家致富。一天，他决定用自己的农具去换镐和铲子。每隔一段时间，他就带他的小驴进迷信山，几天不见踪影。这些山就离我们城市不远。"

马丁内斯老师指着墙上的地图。"人们都传说这个人在这些峡谷中找到了黄金。他时不时地就会从山里出来，总是带着大块大块的真金。人们想跟踪他，但他总是能甩开他们。这个人的名字叫雅各布·瓦尔兹。"

---

pick *n.* 镐

shovel *n.* 铲子

canyon *n.* 峡谷

chunk *n.* 块

"You mean like me?" asked Jacob. The class laughed. Billy looked at his friend and shook his head.

"Kind of like you, Jacob," smiled Mr. Martinez. "Except that he was a farmer, *rancher*, and *miner* who could survive for days in the rough desert."

"I could survive in the rough desert, too," Jacob challenged.

Billy started giggling so hard that his stomach hurt. He took off his big, round glasses to wipe the tears from his eyes. But when he put his glasses back on, things changed from funny to really strange.

"是像我一样的名字？"雅各布问道。全班都笑起来。比利看着他的朋友，摇了摇头。

"是有点像你，雅各布，" 马丁内斯老师笑着说，"除了他是个农民、牧场主还有矿主，并且他能在艰苦的沙漠里待上几天，还能活着出来。"

"我也能在艰苦的沙漠里待上几天，还活着出来。"雅各布挑战道。

比利开始忍不住地咯咯笑，笑到肚子都痛了。他又摘下大圆眼镜，擦他笑出来的眼泪。但是当他重新戴上眼镜时，场面就不再是有趣的课堂，而是变得奇怪了。

---

rancher *n.* 牧场主

miner *n.* 矿主

"As I was saying, Waltz was born in 1810," Mr. Martinez continued. "He died in 1891. Nobody has ever found the ***legendary*** mine. It is probably real, though. I mean, it must be real. It is real. Some people have even been very close to, uh, it."

Mr. Martinez stopped and loosened the top button of his yellow shirt. He ***scratched*** his head a few times. Then he looked around at the class with big wild eyes. Billy had never seen Mr. M. like that before.

"There are still big chunks of gold waiting in those mountains," Mr. Martinez said as he pointed to the map again. He stared at the

---

"就像我刚才说的，瓦尔兹出生于1810年，" 马丁内斯老师继续说。"去世于1891年。没有人找到过那个传说中的金矿。尽管这个传说应该是真的。一定是真的，一定是。有些人曾经非常接近那个地方，嗯，就是那儿。"

马丁内斯老师停下来，解开了他黄色衬衫最上面的扣子。他又挠头挠了几分钟。然后他的大眼睛闪烁着狂热的光芒，把全班扫视了一遍。比利以前从没见过马丁内斯老师这个样子。

"在那些山里还有大块大块的黄金等人们去发现，" 马丁内斯老师说着又指向了那张地图。他盯着那张地图看了很久，但一句话也没说。最

---

legendary *adj.* 传说的

scratch *v.* 抓

map for a long time without saying a word. Finally he turned to the class and said, "Excuse me, but I would like to meet with Jacob and Billy outside, please."

Billy pointed to himself and raised his *eyebrows*. "Yes, you, Billy Smith," repeated Mr. Martinez. "Oh, and Heather, I'd like you to join us as well. Sit tight, class. We'll be back in no time."

Once the four of them were outside of the portable classroom, Mr. Martinez looked a little nervous. His eyes darted from side to side and sweat *dripped* from his forehead. "Heather," he began in a low voice, "I would like you to watch the class for the next few hours."

后他面向全班，说："失陪，但请雅各布和比利到外面来一下。"

比利指了指自己，抬了抬眉毛，感到吃惊。"对，就是你，比利·史密斯，"马丁内斯老师重复了一遍。"哦，还有希瑟，你也出来一下。其他人坐好，我们马上就回来。"

他们四人一到教室的门外，马丁内斯老师就显得很紧张。他的眼睛转来转去，汗滴从他前额落下。"希瑟，"他声音很低地说，"我想让你在接下来的几个小时里，看着全班。"

---

eyebrow *n.* 眉毛　　drip *v.* 滴下

"But, Mr. Martinez, I'm not a teacher!"

"Heather, all you have to do is make sure they don't break anything. You can play heads-up seven-up, hangman, or whatever else you want."

"Could I even ***organize*** a spelling bee?"

"That would be a great idea. Now get going and we'll be back in a while."

Once Heather closed the door, Mr. Martinez turned to Jacob and Billy. "Let's get a move-on, boys! I've got three backpacks in my truck and the afternoon is getting late. Let's hurry before anyone sees us!"

"但是，马丁内斯老师，我又不是老师！"

"希瑟，你要做的就是确保他们不破坏东西。你们可以玩'抬头见喜'、做猜字游戏，想玩什么都行。"

"我们玩拼字比赛也可以吗？"

"玩那个更好了。进去吧，我们一会儿就回来。"

希瑟关上了教室门，马丁内斯老师转向雅各布和比利。"走吧，小伙子们！我的卡车里有三个背包，时间不早了。我们快走，别让别人看见咱们！"

---

organize *v.* 组织；筹备

CHAPTER 2: Mountain Ghosts?

Before Billy realized what was happening, they were at the *outskirts* of the city and climbing into the foothills. He sat in the middle of the truck cab with his arms folded, wondering if he should say anything. Mr. Martinez gripped the steering wheel with two hands and *gazed* straight ahead. Jacob turned his baseball cap backwards and stared out the window.

Finally Jacob turned and asked, "So Mr. M., are we really looking for the gold?" Mr. Martinez grinned and nodded. Then he pressed down even harder on the gas pedal.

"Holy geezgrubbers!" Billy blurted out. "But, but, it's just a

---

第二章：山上有鬼？

比利还没弄清楚怎么回事，他们就已经到了市郊，卡车开始上山。他坐在卡车车厢的中间，双手交叉，在想是不是应该说点什么。马丁内斯老师双手紧握方向盘，目光直视前方。雅各布把棒球帽帽檐转到脑后，盯着窗外看。

最终雅各布转身过来，问："那么，马丁老师，我们真的是去找黄金吗？"老师笑着点点头，然后加大了油门。

"我的神仙上帝呀！"比利大喊出声。"但是，但是，那只是个传说，一个古老的故事而已——别人会到处找我们的。"他看了看表。"已

---

outskirt *n.* 郊区

gaze *v.* 注视

legend, an old story—and they're going to look for us." He looked down at his watch. "It's already three o'clock. My mom is waiting for me in front of the principal's office right now!"

"They say that Waltz entered these mountains through Boulder Canyon," Mr. Martinez said as he pointed off to the right. "That's where we'll start. Are you in, Jacob?"

Jacob nodded. "Yep, and so is our friend here," he said as he *slapped* Billy on the back.

"Good," said Mr. Martinez, "because there's a rumor that a few people have *spotted* Waltz up here in the past few weeks. With things heating up again, this should be an ideal time to go." Their

---

经三点了。妈妈正在校长办公室前面等我呢！"

"他们说瓦尔兹就是通过波尔德峡谷进入那些山里的，" 马丁内斯老师指着右边说道。"我们就从那开始走。你来不来，雅各布？"

雅各布点点头。"我去，我们这个朋友也去，"他说着拍了拍比利的后背。

"很好，"马丁内斯老师说，"因为有传言说，有几个人几周前在这儿见到了瓦尔兹。人们又不断地提起这件事，现在去肯定是个好时候。"卡车突然转向一条颠簸不平、灰尘弥漫的路上。马丁内斯老师继续加速，

---

slap *v.* 拍打

spot *v.* 发现

truck *veered* off onto a *bumpy*, dirt road. Mr. Martinez sped up, leaving a dust cloud streaming behind them.

"Are you talking ghosts?" Billy needed to know. "Because Jacob Waltz would be 192 years old!"

"Call it what you wish, my friend, but the ghost will help us find the gold."

"Oh gosh," Billy sighed as he slapped his forehead in disbelief. "They've gone mad, absolutely *bonkers*! I'll bet it's gold fever. We should be at school right now — they'll start looking for us!"

"Wait, maybe we should go to the doctor first. I've read about

---

整个车后面尘土飞扬。

"你是说有鬼吗？"比利很想知道。"因为雅各布·瓦尔兹还活着的话，已经192岁了！"

"你想怎么叫就怎么叫吧，我的朋友，但是鬼会帮我们找到黄金的。"

"天哪，"比利很是怀疑地拍着脑门，长声叹气。"这些人一定是疯了，绝对是疯子！我敢说，这就是想黄金想疯了。我们现在应该在学校才对——其他人一定在找我们！"

"等等，也许我们应该先去医院。我在网上读到过关于淘金热的消

---

veer *v.* 转向

bumpy *adj.* 颠簸的

bonkers *n.* 疯子

gold fever on the Internet. They say people start acting funny when they think they're close to finding gold. Their eyes get big and yellow, and they start scratching their heads a lot. They can even laugh for over ten seconds at nothing at all."

Billy stopped talking because he could tell they were not listening. Mr. Martinez carefully pulled the truck off the right-hand side of the road and parked it behind two mesquite trees. "There, that should hide us," he said. "Could you guys grab the packs out of the back?"

Jacob and Billy opened up the *tailgate* and saw three different colored backpacks. "The green one is for you Jacob," Mr. Martinez

息。据说人们在觉得自己马上找到黄金的时候行为都非常可笑。他们的眼睛会睁大，而且泛黄，经常会不断地挠头。什么事都没有，他们也能大笑十秒钟以上。"

比利住嘴不说了，因为他发现那两个人根本没听他说话。马丁内斯老师小心地把车停到路的右手边，在两棵灌木的中间。"停这吧，应该能帮我们藏身，"他说。"你们俩能去后面把背包拿出来吗？"

雅各布和比利打开车的后挡板，看见三个不同颜色的背包。"绿色的是给你的，雅各布，" 马丁内斯老师喊道，"把蓝的给比利，那个大的是我的。"

tailgate *n.* 后挡板

called. "Hand the blue pack to Billy, and I'll take the big one."

Billy looked inside his blue backpack. He found a flashlight, two cans of beans, a full canteen, a musty pillow, and an old Mexican blanket. At the bottom he saw a long steel hunting knife. "So, Mr. Martinez," Billy called as he held up the knife, "is this so I can kill a ghost?"

Mr. Martinez looked at Jacob and then at Billy. "All right Billy, here's the deal: you can either come along *willingly*—"

"Willingly? But you dragged me out here!"

"You can either come along willingly," repeated Mr. Martinez, "or you can stay here and *guard* the truck. This is an important trip, and

---

比利看了看他的蓝色背包里面，有一只手电筒、两盒豆子、一只装满水的水壶、一个发霉的枕头，还有一条很旧的墨西哥毛毯。在背包最下面，他看见一把很长的捕猎钢刀。"那么，马丁内斯老师，"比利抓住那把刀喊道，"我用这个就可以把鬼杀死了吗？"

马丁内斯老师看看雅各布又看看比利。"好了比利，事情就是这样：你可以自愿加入我们——"

"自愿？但是是你把我拉到这儿来的！"

"你可以自愿和我们一起去，"马丁内斯老师重复道，"你也可以待在这儿看着卡车。这次行程很重要，所以我和雅各布希望你能一起来——

---

willingly *adv.* 自愿地　　guard *v.* 看守

Jacob and I would like you to come along—but only if you are not going to complain."

Billy looked around him at the Sonoran Desert. There were no stores, no people, and no paved roads in sight. There were just sharp *cacti*, loose rocks, steep mountains, and a *scorching* sun. He knew that *rattlesnakes*, *scorpions*, coyotes, and Gila monsters roamed this desert. Maybe even mountain lions lived nearby.

Billy swung the pack over his shoulder. "I'll come," he said.

"Good," responded Mr. Martinez, without breaking a smile. "The knife is not to stab anybody. Knives can be used for cooking, whittling wood, or hunting."

但是你来了就不能再啰嗦。"

比利看了看所在的索诺兰沙漠——没有商店、没有人，视野所及连条路都没有。有的只是带刺的仙人掌、散落的石头、险峻的山脉和酷热的太阳。他知道响尾蛇、蝎子、土狼和毒蜥都会在此出没。甚至附近还可能有美洲狮。

比利把背包甩到背后。"我和你们去，"他说。

"很好，"马丁内斯老师不动声色地答道，"刀不是用来伤人的。刀可以用来做饭、削木头，或者捕猎。"

---

cacti *n.* 仙人掌

rattlesnake *n.* 响尾蛇

scorching *adj.* 炽热的

scorpion *n.* 蝎子

Mr. Martinez locked the doors of his truck and looked around to see if anybody was watching. Then he lowered his hat and looked up in the direction of the sun. "We've got a few good hours to get past the first ridge," he said, pointing high up into the mountains.

Billy looked back at the distant city and pointed to the storm clouds on the *horizon*. "Do you think that's a *monsoon* storm coming this way?" Billy wondered out loud.

"We're going, Billy!" Jacob called from the trailhead. "Storm or no storm, we are going to find the lost gold mine." Jacob turned and started up the trail. Mr. Martinez followed him without saying a word.

马丁内斯老师锁上了卡车门，又四下看了看有没有人偷看他们。然后他把帽檐压低，看了看太阳。“我们还有好一段时间来爬过第一道山脊，”他说着，指向远方山脉的高处。

比利回头看着遥远的城市，指着地平线上升起的乌云。“那是季风暴雨朝这边来了吗？”比利不禁问出了声。

“往前走了，比利！”雅各布在小路路口那里喊他。“不管有没有暴风雨，我们都要去寻找那座迷失的金矿。”雅各布转过身，沿着小路走过去。马丁内斯老师跟在他后面走，一语不发。

---

horizon *n.* 地平线

monsoon *n.* 雨季；季风

Billy looked down at his dusty new shoes. Everything seemed dusty out here. Billy took off his big glasses and wiped them with his shirt. When he put them back on, Jacob and Mr. Martinez were already out of sight. Billy took one final look back at the city, tightened up his pack, and ran after them up the desert *trail*.

CHAPTER 3: Camp Coyote

The hiking trail was only wide enough for one person at a time. It wound back and forth through the *foothills* and over dry washes. Next to the trail, old saguaro cacti stood like the gatekeepers of

比利低头看了看他的新鞋，现在也满是灰尘。这里的一切都布满了灰尘。比利摘下眼镜，用衬衫擦了擦。等他戴上眼镜时，雅各布和马丁内斯老师已经不见踪影了。比利最后回头看了一眼城市，然后拉紧背包，沿着那条沙漠小路跑着追了过去。

第三章：营地土狼

他们所走的小路很窄，一次只能容一人通过。小路绵延曲折，穿过小山丘，经过干涸的洼地。小路旁边，生长多年的巨大仙人掌像门卫一样保护着这些山脉。这三位淘金者默默地穿过了第一条山脊，进入了波尔德峡

trail *n.* 小路　　foothill *n.* 小丘

these desert mountains. The three gold-seekers traveled in silence over the first ridge, dipped down into Boulder Canyon, and lost sight of the city behind them. Except for two quick pee breaks, they kept a steady pace.

"This looks like a good place to spend the night," Mr. Martinez said at last. He pointed up at a tall, narrow peak. "That's Weaver's Needle, where there have been reports of ..." He stopped in mid-sentence. "That is where we will find the gold *mine* tomorrow. Let's set up camp."

Billy wondered what camp there was to set up. He had no

谷，已经完全看不见城市了。他们始终匀速前行，中途只短暂地休息过两次。

“这看起来是个过夜的好地方，” 马丁内斯老师终于说道。他指着远方一处又高又窄的山峰。“那就是‘织补针’峰，传言就是说在那……”他话到中途停了一下。“那就是我们明天会发现金矿的地方。我们先安营吧。”

比利在想能搭起什么样的宿营地。他背包里没有睡袋，他们三人好像也没有谁带了帐篷。他拽出枕头和毛毯，铺在雅克布的毛毯旁边。雅克布

---

mine *n.* 矿山

sleeping bag in his pack, and nobody seemed to have a tent. He pulled out the pillow and blanket, and laid them down near Jacob's blanket. Jacob was busy *rearranging* some stones into a circle.

"Was that somebody's *campfire*?" Billy asked him.

"Must have been," Jacob replied without looking up. "Probably somebody else looking for the gold a long time ago." Jacob stopped piling rocks and held his hand up. "Ahh, that breeze feels mmm mmm good." He took off his sweaty Phoenix Suns T-shirt and hung it on a tree branch.

"Mr. M., do you think a monsoon storm is coming?" Billy worried.

正忙着把一些石头排成一圈。

“那是有人点起的篝火吗？”比利问他。

“一定是，”雅克布头也不抬地答道，“可能很久以前就有人来这找黄金了。” 雅克布摆完了石头，把手举了起来。“啊，这风吹得……嗯……太舒服了。”他把自己被汗湿透的菲尼克斯太阳队T恤衫脱了下来，挂在树枝上。

“马丁老师，你说是不是季风暴雨要来了？”比利担心地问道。

---

rearrange *v.* 重新布置

campfire *n.* 篝火

Mr. Martinez looked up from his blanket. "Yeah, could be. The air is starting to *swirl*. But don't worry, Billy. See that rocky ledge up there? If the rain starts coming down hard, we'll be up there in two minutes."

By the time it got dark, Mr. Martinez had started a fire. The dried branches quickly burned and became bright orange coals inside the stone circle. Mr. Martinez rested an old pot across two of the stones. He poured in three cans of beans and blew on the coals. Soon yellow flames danced around the pot. The three stared silently into the *mesmerizing* fire.

马丁内斯老师在毛毯上抬头看了看。“是，可能是。开始出现气旋了。但是比利，不用担心。看见那块突出的岩石了吗？要是雨真下大了，我们用不上两分钟就能跑到那儿。”

天黑的时候，马丁内斯老师点起火来。干枯的树枝很快燃起来，在石头堆成的圈子里烧成了亮桔色的木炭。马丁内斯老师在其中的两块石头上放了一个旧锅。他倒进去三罐豆子，又给火堆扇风。不一会锅边就都是黄色的火苗了。三个人无言地看着仿佛会迷惑人的火焰。

swirl *v.* 打旋

mesmerizing *adj.* 迷人的

"Mr. Martinez," Jacob began, "you never finished telling our class about the end of the legend. What happened to the Lost Dutchman?"

"Where did I leave off?" Mr. Martinez wanted to know.

Billy looked up. "You said that he used to disappear into the mountains-these mountains. And he would come back into the city with gold a few days later. So people tried to follow him, but he always gave them the *slip*. That's where you stopped."

Mr. Martinez was still staring into the flames. "He died in his house with a box of gold under his bed."

"马丁内斯老师，"雅各布说道，"你一直都没给同学们讲那个传说的结尾。那个'迷失的荷兰人'后来怎么样了？"

"我讲到哪了？"马丁内斯老师不记得了。

比利抬起头来。"你说他总是进山之后就消失不见了——就是这些山。然后他几天后回到城市，总是带着很多黄金。所以人们想跟着他，但他总能把大家甩开。就说到这。"

马丁内斯老师还在盯着火焰看。"他死在自己家里，死的时候床下还有一袋黄金。"

slip *n.* 逃离

"His friends asked him where the gold mine was, but he never really told them. They tried to find it for years, but never could."

"So, Mr. M.," Billy said *delicately*, "if Jacob Waltz died over 100 years ago, how have people seen him up here in the past few weeks?"

Mr. Martinez had that strange look in his eye again. Jacob sat up on his blanket. He and Billy waited for an answer. Mr. Martinez studied their faces, as if wondering how much he should tell them.

"Okay," he said at last, "I'll tell you what I know. For over 100 years, people have come to these mountains in search of this mine. Everybody has their *theories*. Some believe Waltz hid the entrance

---

"他的朋友们问过他金矿在哪，但他从来没说过实话。他们找了很多年，但一直都没找到。"

"所以，马丁老师，"比利小心翼翼地问道，"如果雅克布・瓦尔兹一百多年前就死了，怎么最近几周还会有人看见他了呢？"

马丁内斯老师又露出了奇怪的眼神。雅克布从毯子上坐了起来。他和比利都在等老师的回答。马丁内斯老师反复看着他们的脸，好像在想应不应该告诉他们。

"好吧，"他最终说，"我就把我知道的告诉你们。一百多年以前，人们来到这些山里来寻找金矿。大家说法不一，有人说瓦尔兹藏身在有岩

---

delicately *adv.* 小心翼翼地　　theory *n.* （未证明的）意见；看法

with rocks. Others believe an earthquake covered it up. *Skeptics* claim that it is just a *myth*. Other people believe it only opens at certain times of the year."

"How so?" inquired Jacob.

"Funny things happen with these monsoon storms," Mr. Martinez said as he looked up at the clouds overhead. "It's like there's electricity in the air. Monsoons are so powerful that they can scramble things — like time."

"Scramble time?" blurted Billy in disbelief. "What exactly does that mean?"

石的入口那；还有人认为地震把金矿埋起来了；怀疑论者认为这只是个神话；也有人认为金矿一年只开放几次而已。"

"怎么会是这样呢？"雅各布问道。

"就是这些季风暴雨使事情有趣起来，" 马丁内斯老师说着，又抬起头看头顶的云团。"这就像空气中有电流一样。季风的威力大到可以扰乱很多东西——比如说时间。"

"扰乱时间？"比利满是怀疑地插嘴道。"那是什么意思？"

---

skeptic *n.* 怀疑论者

myth *n.* 神话

Mr. Martinez *poked* a stick into the coals. "During the stormy season, *portals* open up to different time periods. They are like doorways to the past and the future. During this scrambled time, our paths could cross with somebody from the past."

"And that is how you think people have seen Jacob Waltz recently," Jacob added.

Mr. Martinez nodded. "There has been pretty amazing proof lately. My brother-in-law and a friend were hiking here two weeks ago. Through their *binoculars*, they saw a man walking high up near Weaver's Needle. There was a *burro* walking behind him."

马丁内斯老师用木棍捅着木炭。"在暴风季节，有很多个入口通向不同的时间段，就像是通向过去和未来的通道。在这些打乱的时间里，我们在路上就可能和过去的某个人相遇。"

"这就是你为什么相信最近有人见过雅各布·瓦尔兹了，"雅各布说。

马丁内斯老师点点头。"最近有很多令人称奇的证据出现。我的妹夫和他一个朋友两周以前到这来过。他们通过望远镜看到有人在'织补针'的高处附近行走，在他身后有一头小驴。"

---

poke *v.* 捅　　portal *n.* 入口

binoculars *n.* 双筒望远镜　　burro *n.* 小驴

Mr. Martinez looked at the two boys. The yellowish color of the fire reflected in his eyes. “And on the next day, they found a *nugget* of gold on the trail,” he whispered. “It was the size of a baseball.”

Jacob whistled. Billy pulled the blanket farther over his shoulders.

“Tomorrow morning, we will forget the trail and follow that wash. It heads up the canyon to the base of Weaver’s Needle.” Mr. Martinez stopped to listen. One howl turned into a chorus of yapping and howling. “Yes, Billy, there are *coyotes* out here. But they don’t go after people. They’ve probably just killed a deer — that’s all.”

马丁内斯老师看着这两个男孩。黄色的火焰反射在他的眼睛里。“然后第二天，他们在路上发现了一块天然的黄金，”他低声说道。“有棒球那么大。”

雅各布吹了声口哨。比利把毯子向上拉，拉到肩膀上面。

“明天早上，我们就不走这条路了，沿着洼地走。那样可以直接进入峡谷，到‘织补针’的山脚下。” 马丁内斯老师停下来，聆听着什么。一声嚎叫引起了一群乱吠和嚎叫。“是的，比利，这附近有土狼。但他们不会伤人。他们至多就是杀死只麋鹿。”

---

nugget *n.* 天然金块

coyote *n.* 土狼

CHAPTER 4: The Next Day

Billy heard some *rustling* noises. For a moment his whole body froze. He slowly opened his eyes. Mr. Martinez was breaking sticks and putting them into the fire.

Billy quietly rolled his eyes up toward the desert sky. The sun was not up yet, but the dawn's light was turning the sky from black to light blue. Billy's body ached from sleeping on the ground. His body and blanket smelled like dirt. He could even taste it on his lips.

The three gold seekers ate a quick bowl of *oatmeal* and packed up camp. They headed up the wash before the sun's rays could peak

---

第四章：次日

比利听到了一些沙沙的响声。有一瞬间，他全身都冻僵了。他慢慢地睁开眼睛。看到马丁内斯老师正在折断木棍，把火烧旺些。

比利默默地抬眼向沙漠上方的天空望去。太阳还没升起，但是黎明的光亮使天空从黑色变为浅蓝。比利在地上睡了这一觉，全身酸痛。他身上和毯子上都是泥土味。他甚至还用嘴唇试了一下味道。

这三位淘金者快速地吃了碗麦片，就打包行李。他们在阳光还没照到险峻的峡谷石壁上时，就向洼地出发了。马丁内斯老师走得很快，不太讲话。比利很担心，因为他又在老师的眼睛里看到了那种疯狂的神色——比

---

rustling *n.* 沙沙声　　oatmeal *n.* 麦片

over the steep canyon walls. Mr. Martinez walked quickly and didn't speak much. Billy was worried because he had that crazy look in his eyes — even scarier than the day before.

By noon, they were hot and sweaty. The temperature was well over 100 degrees F. Billy's feet ached. When they finally stopped for lunch, Mr. Martinez passed the *canteen* around. "Keep yourselves *hydrated* boys," he said, "because there's no telling how fast we might have to run down this hill!"

Mr. Martinez looked over at them and laughed for at least ten seconds. Then he scratched his head and laughed some more. Billy

---

前一天更加可怕了。

到了中午，他们感觉很热，汗流浃背。气温超过了100华氏度。比利的双脚疼痛。终于停下来吃午饭了，马丁内斯老师让大家传着水壶喝水。“孩子们，身体里始终要有水分，”他说，“因为没人知道我们跑下山还有多远的路！”

马丁内斯老师看着他们，笑了至少有十秒钟。然后他开始挠头，笑得时间更长了。比利看看雅各布，看见他也在笑。雅各布的眼神里也出现了那种好笑的神色。

---

canteen *n.* 水壶

hydrated *adj.* 含水的

looked over at Jacob and saw that he was laughing, too. Jacob also seemed to have that funny look in his eyes.

Suddenly Jacob began to sing, "We're going to get rich today, la-da-dee-dee-da-da! And no more bills to pay, la-dee-dee-dee-da!" He stopped for just a moment. "Hey Billy, I'll buy you a new bike tomorrow! Do you want a mountain bike or a motorcycle?" Mr. Martinez laughed, and Jacob *shrieked* again. Then Jacob started to scratch his head, too.

By mid-afternoon they were getting so close they could feel it. Jacob had stopped singing and Mr. Martinez *scanned* the

突然雅各布开始唱歌，“我们今天就发财，啦哒滴滴答答！再也不用付账单，啦哒滴滴答答！”他停了一会。“喂，比利，我明天给你买一辆新自行车！你想要山地车还是电动车？”马丁内斯老师笑起来，雅各布又发出尖叫，然后雅各布也开始挠头了。

下午过半，他们离目的地非常接近，几乎感觉到了那里的气息。雅各布不再唱歌，马丁内斯老师也搜索着山边看有没有线索。比利小心地看着双脚，不要踩到小树枝。

shriek *v.* 发出尖叫声

scan *v.* 细看；察看

mountainside for *clues*. Billy watched his feet carefully and tried not to step on any *twigs*.

As the hour went on, the air began to swirl. Small clouds from the horizon were now big, black, and rumbling overhead. There was almost a sweet smell to the air. Suddenly Jacob stopped and shouted, "I saw it, I saw it, I saw him!"

Mr. Martinez quickly put his hand over Jacob's mouth. "Shhh, shhhhh ... that's better," he said. Mr. M.'s golden eyes looked into Jacob's golden eyes. "This should be about the right time. Now tell me, Jacob, where did you see him?"

Jacob pointed up to a pile of fallen rocks at the eastern base of

---

时间一点点过去，又出现了气旋。天边的小云团现在变得又大又黑，在他们头顶轰隆作响。空气中甚至有点甜甜的气味。突然间雅各布停住脚步，大声喊道："我看见了，我看见了，我看见他了！"

马丁内斯老师把手压在雅各布嘴上。"嘘，嘘……看见最好，"他说。马丁老师的金色眼睛直直地向雅各布的金色眼睛看过去。"差不多就是这个时候了。现在告诉我，雅各布，你在哪看见他的？"

雅各布指向"织补针"东部盆地一堆滚落的岩石上。马丁内斯老师从

---

clue *n.* 线索　　twig *n.* 细枝

Weaver's Needle. Mr. Martinez looked through his binoculars and smiled from ear to ear. "Well, I'll be! There's Wickety, the old man's burro." Billy looked up at Mr. M.'s big smile *underneath* the binoculars. His teacher was missing two teeth on the right side.

When a few big drops of rain fell, Mr. Martinez put the binoculars down. "Okay, guys, let's huddle up," he said. "This is a dream that is over 100 years old. This legend is real, and we will become its final chapter. We are going into the mine to stuff as much gold as will fit into our backpacks. If we get split up, we'll meet back at the truck."

"But which way is the truck?" Billy asked.

他的望远镜看过去，笑得嘴都快咧开了。"是，不错！就是那个老头的小毛驴。"比利抬头看着马丁老师在望远镜下露出的夸张笑容。他的老师嘴的右边缺了两颗牙齿。

几滴大雨点从天而降，马丁内斯老师放下了望远镜。"好了，小伙子们，我们抱在一起吧，"他说。"这个梦人们已经做了一百年了。这个传说是真的，我们就来为这个故事收尾。我们要到金矿里去，把我们的背包都装满黄金。如果我们一会走散了，就回到卡车那里见面。"

"但是回卡车怎么走？"比利问道。

---

underneath *prep.* 在下面

"That way," Mr. Martinez pointed. "Just follow the wash—and if you don't see the truck, just keep going downhill. From there, you can hitch a ride into town." He paused and leaned down close to Billy's face. "But don't tell anybody about the gold."

"What will we do inside the mine?" Jacob needed to know. "What if he's in there?"

Mr. Martinez glanced down at the knife *strapped* to his *belt*. "We'll be fine," he answered. "There are three of us. Now empty out your packs. Let's *stash* everything behind these trees."

"那边，"马丁内斯老师指了一下。"就沿着洼地走——如果看不见卡车，就一直沿着下山的路走。从那，你就能够搭上便车回城里去。"他说完了，俯身下来贴近比利的脸。"但是不要对任何人讲黄金的事。"

"我们在金矿里怎么做？"雅各布很想知道。"他要是在里面怎么办？"

马丁内斯老师低头看了看腰带里拴着的刀。"我们不会有事的，"他答道。"我们有三个人呢。现在把你们的背包清空。把东西藏到树后去。"

---

strap *v.* 绑

stash *v.* 存放

belt *n.* 腰带

More big raindrops started to fall. Billy tucked his musty pillow and Mexican blanket under some rocks. "The food and water, too, Billy," Mr. Martinez instructed him.

"But Mr. Martinez, what if we get hungry or *dehydrated*?"

"Billy, we need room for the gold," Jacob explained.

"Do bring the flashlights though," whispered Mr. Martinez. "It'll be dark inside."

CHAPTER 5: The Gold Mine

At the mine's entrance, the old burro was tied to a rock. The tattered rope was fastened around her neck by just one loose *knot*.

雨下得更大了。比利把发霉的枕头和墨西哥毛毯塞到了一些岩石下面。"把食物和水也放在那，比利，" 马丁内斯老师指示道。

"但是马丁内斯老师，我们要是饿了或者缺水了怎么办？"

"比利，我们需要地方来放黄金，" 雅各布解释说。

"但一定要带上手电筒，" 马丁内斯老师低声说。"里面一定很黑。"

第五章：金矿

在矿山的入口，一头很老的毛驴拴在一块岩石上。它脖子上绑着一条

---

dehydrated *adj.* 缺水的

knot *n.* 结

The burro's grayish coat looked as if it had spent many days in the desert sun. Her ancient face turned to watch the three approaching gold seekers. She *stomped* her *hoof* into the dirt.

"Easy there, Wickety," whispered Mr. Martinez, placing a hand on her head. He pulled some oats out of his front pocket. Wickety ate them from his hand. Mr. Martinez gave her a final pat and motioned the boys toward the entrance.

Inside the mine, it was dark. Mr. Martinez, Jacob, and Billy stood in the entrance room, waiting for their eyes to adjust. Slowly they could make out two tunnels: one straight ahead and one to the right. An old shovel and pick leaned against one wall.

破烂的绳子，只打了一个很松的结。驴子全身的毛都发灰，好像在沙漠的烈日下待了好多天了。它那苍老的脸转过来看着这三位正在走近的淘金者。把蹄子重重地踩进了土里。

“放松点，小驴，” 马丁内斯老师轻声说着，把手放在驴头上。他从前面衣袋里掏出一些麦片放在手掌。小驴吃了下去。马丁内斯老师最后拍了它一下，然后打手势示意两个孩子进去。

进到矿里面，一片黑暗。马丁内斯老师、雅各布和比利站在入口处，让眼睛适应一下。渐渐地，他们看到了两条通道：一条在中间，一条在右手边。一把铲子和一把镐靠着一侧墙立着。

---

stomp *v.* 跺脚　　hoof *n.* 蹄子

"I'll go straight ahead, and you two go right," Mr. Martinez whispered. "We'll meet out front by the burro."

"I'm not going," said Billy. "I'm afraid of the dark!"

"Then you don't get any gold," Jacob *threatened*.

Billy looked at Jacob and then at Mr. Martinez. Their eyes glowed a soft yellow in the dark cave. "I'm not going," he repeated.

Mr. Martinez shook his head. "Okay Jacob, let's both try the center tunnel then."

Before Billy knew it, his teacher and friend had disappeared into the darkness. After a moment, he could no longer hear their

---

"我走中间这条，你们俩走右手边，"马丁内斯老师轻声嘱咐，"我们一会回到驴子那里见。"

"我不去，"比利说。"我怕黑！"

"那你就分不到黄金，"雅各布威胁他说。

比利看了看雅各布又看了看马丁内斯老师。他们两人的眼神在黑暗的洞穴里流露出了柔和的黄色光芒。"我不去，"他重复了一遍。

马丁内斯老师摇了摇头。"好吧，雅各布，那咱们俩就走中间这条通道吧。"

比利还没看清楚，他的老师和朋友就消失在黑暗中了。过了一会，他

---

threaten *v.* 威胁；恐吓

footsteps. Billy's throat sank down to the bottom of his stomach. He gulped and leapt out into the light.

It was raining hard now. Billy could see lightning strike the desert floor miles away. In the far distance, he could see the lights of Phoenix slowly turning on for the evening. Billy thought of his mom and wondered if his school photo was already on milk cartons.

Wickety was getting ***soaked***. Billy thought she seemed sad, so he walked over to her. "Sweetie, are you for real?" he asked before patting her head. "Are you really from the nineteenth century? Would you like to run free into the desert?" Billy started to loosen the rope around her neck.

连他们的脚步声都听不到了。比利的心提到了嗓子眼。他喘着气大步跑到了光亮处。

雨下得很大。在几英里外沙漠上的，比利都看得见。在远处，他能看见菲尼克斯城夜晚的灯光一点点亮起。比利想到了妈妈，还想他在学校的照片是不是已经印在牛奶纸盒上了。

小驴全身都湿透了。比利觉得它看起来很伤心，就向它走过去。“亲爱的，你是真的吗？”他问道，又拍了拍它的头。“你真是从19世纪来的吗？你想去沙漠里自由地奔跑吗？”比利开始给它解开脖子上的绳子。

---

soak *v.* 使湿透

But just then he heard a shout from the mine. Billy ran into the entrance room and waited for his eyes to adjust. He heard Mr. M's voice, and it sounded happy. "Gold, gold, gold!" *echoed* throughout the mine.

Billy cringed. "Be quiet, you guys!" he screamed down the tunnel. "He could hear you!"

And then Billy turned toward the footsteps. They were coming from the tunnel to the right. He looked down and only saw the shovel leaning against the wall. He picked it up.

From the dark shadows, a face *emerged*. The face looked like old

---

但是这时，他听到矿里传出了 一声大叫。比利跑到入口去让眼睛适应一下黑暗。他听到了马丁内斯老师的声音，他听起来很高兴。“黄金，黄金，黄金！”他的喊声在矿内引起了回音。

比利有点畏缩了。“你们俩，安静点！”他朝着通道大声喊，“他能听见你们说话！”

然后比利就朝着脚步声走过去。他们是从右边的通道回来的。他向里面看，只看见墙边立着的铲子。就捡了起来。

在黑暗中，出现了一个人的脸。这张脸看起来像张旧皮革。眼睛旁边都是深深的皱纹，像一个一百岁的老人。他的嘴张开了，露出了夸张而恐

---

echo *v.* 发回声　　emerge *v.* 出现

leather. Deep lines circled two eyes that seemed a century old. Its mouth opened into a big, scary smile and a gold tooth reflected the day's *final* light behind Billy. Billy gulped. "Jacob?" he said in a weak voice as he dropped the shovel. "Jacob, is that you?"

"Shhhh," came a voice.

"Jacob, I didn't do it!" he shouted. "I don't care about the gold—I just want to go home to my mommy!"

And the class laughed. Everybody was looking at him.

"Billy, are you okay?" Mr. Martinez asked. Billy looked up and nodded. "Good, because you can talk to Jacob about gold after

---

怖的笑容，一颗金牙上反射着比利身后的最后一缕阳光。比利倒吸了一口冷气。“雅各布？”他扔掉了铲子，用微弱的声音问道。“雅各布，真的是你吗？”

“嘘！”有个声音说。

“雅各布，我什么都没做！”他大喊道。“我不在乎什么黄金——我只想回家找妈妈！”

全班都大笑起来。所有人都看着他。

“比利，你还好吗？” 马丁内斯老师问道。比利抬起头，又点了点头。“很好，因为你可以课后和雅各布讨论黄金的事。现在我们讨论的是

---

final *adj.* 最终的；最后的

class. Right now, we are talking about Arizona in the early 1900s. Let's see, where were we?"

"You just said that, in 1912, Arizona became the forty-eighth state," Jacob said. "Before that, you talked about gold seekers in the desert mountains."

"Thank you, Jacob," said Mr. Martinez. "If you keep that up, you may get an A in this class after all."

Jacob smiled and then looked over at Billy. "Are you crazy, *amigo*?" he whispered.

Billy looked down, *embarrassed*. This wasn't the first time he had

---

20世纪早期亚利桑那州的情况。看一下，我们讲到哪了？"

"你刚刚说到，1912年，亚利桑那成为第48个州，"雅克布说道。"之前，你说的是关于在沙漠山地有淘金者的事情。"

"谢谢你，雅各布，" 马丁内斯老师说。"如果你一直这么专心，你到期末这门课会得A的。"

雅各布笑笑，然后看着比利。"你疯了吗，我的朋友？"他轻声说。

比利看着脚下，十分窘迫。这已经不是他第一次在课堂上睡着做梦了。"我也不知道，"他答道。

---

amigo *n.* 朋友（源于西班牙语amigo） embarrassed *adj.* 窘迫的

daydreamed in class. "I don't know," he answered.

Heather *yawned* in the seat in front of him. From her stretching arms, a note landed on Billy's desk: "If you strike it rich, let us know. Love, Heather."

She started laughing. Billy saw that Jacob was laughing, too. But when Jacob turned around, he seemed to have that strange look in his eyes again. Billy looked down at Jacob's sneakers and stopped. They were unusually dusty. And there were cactus thorns in the soles.

希瑟在他前面的座位上伸着懒腰。一张纸条从她伸出的手里落到比利的桌上，上面写着："如果你发达了，要告诉我们。你的好朋友：希瑟。"

她开始笑起来。比利看见雅各布也在笑。但是当雅各布转身的时候，他又在他的眼睛里看见了那种怪异的眼神。比利低头看着雅各布的鞋子，愣住了。雅各布的鞋子特别脏。在脚底还有仙人掌的刺。

---

yawn *v.* 打哈欠

"Jacob! Billy! Heather!" Mr. Martinez said in an *exasperated* tone. "I'm trying to teach class here. What should I do with you three?" He scratched his head without saying anything. Then he scratched his head some more.

"I'd like to see you three outside," he said at last. "The rest of you sit tight. We'll be back in no time."

"雅各布！比利！希瑟！" 马丁内斯老师听起来有点生气。"我正在上课呢，得拿你们三个怎么办？" 他不说话了，开始挠头，挠了又挠。

"你们三个到教室门口来，" 他最后说。"其他人坐好。我们一会就回来。"

---

exasperated *adj.* 恼怒的